Where The Tourists Leave

A NOVEL BY MEGAN & JONATHAN RIFF

WHEN THE TOURISTS LEAVE
A NOVEL

COPYRIGHT ©2021 BY MEGAN & JONATHAN RIFF
PUBLISHED IN THE UNITED STATES BY CAPTAINS &
COWBOYS

I S B N - 9780578307022

www.WhenTheTouristsLeave.com

Jonathan@CaptainsandCowboys.com
Megan@CaptainsandCowboys.com

INSTAGRAM
@CaptSteezy
@MRiff_Daily
@WhenTheTouristsLeave

YOUTUBE
JonathanRiffWeekly

DISCLAIMER

This book is a memoir. It reflects both of the author's recollections of experiences over time. Events have been compressed, and some dialogue has been recreated. We changed the names of some nice people to maintain their privacy. We changed the names of some bad people, but you know who you are.

The reader should also be aware that the authors have been corrected on some points, mostly regarding Croatian jokes - especially ones involving your mother. We've allowed some of these points to stay, as this is a memoir, and memories tell their own stories.

This book is a reflection of our story and we've done our best to make it a truthful story. The views and opinions expressed within this novel are those of the authors only and do not necessarily reflect or represent the views and opinions held by individuals or institutions on which our characters are based.

BASED ON A TRUE STORY

PROLOGUE

In November of 2017, my husband was hit with warm watermelon juice. He was standing waist-deep in the plunge pool attached to our room when he got covered with the stuff. It arrived fast and hard, leaving his torso dotted with tiny red chunks and his skin blushed. Megan is my name and I remember watching as little pink rivers rolled south into the water while he stood in silent shock. I'd never gotten sick on Jonathan before. Never thrown up on anyone.

You might not expect to read that kind of thing on the first page of a book. After all, this is the story about a couple Americans who opened a boutique hotel in an old Communist Party meeting house in Eastern Europe.

Right?

Right.

But the moment I'm talking about is important. Our lives changed forever that day, when my world, our world, flipped upside down and never flipped back. This story is about what led to that moment and what we did afterwards.

Jonathan and I were on our honeymoon. In Phuket, Thailand. No one would want their trip to be one they'd remember for the wrong reasons. But we got some bad news. We knew it was a possibility that we would get that news and had braced ourselves for it.

Then it became real.

Please don't think I'm exaggerating. I would've done a lot to avoid getting sick on my husband of only six weeks. But that's what happened when we got the news. In a half second, my vision smudged, and my brain lost its way. My physiological response was to hit, eject.

Think about working harder than you ever have for something, for longer than you thought you ever could. Think about giving it every inch of your mind, every ounce of your energy. Imagine leaving your home for it, changing your career for it, saying goodbye to your friends and family and colleagues and country for it. Imagine being unable to sleep over it, cry over it, feel like you're losing your mind over it.

Understand how it could become an obsession. How the longer it went on, the harder it was to quit. How the tougher it became, the more I needed to fight.

And you do fight. You don't quit. You do start to get there. You do start to win.

It'll leave you broken, crazy, and exhausted, but you know you're doing a good thing, that people love what you're achieving. You reach a point where it all feels worth the risk and the time and the upheaval. You start to feel it has been worth all the sweat and tears and heart and soul and DNA you buried right into it. It gets to an incredible point where you can call it a success, no question.

And then, just when your dream becomes reality, you learn that what you thought you knew was never true. In the blink of an eye, that dream can be snatched away in circumstances so cloudy you want to scream your lungs out.

That's how it felt then, how it feels right now, and how it felt the day my light lunch hit my husband.

Our dream was brought to life for the greatest of reasons, and in the end, killed off for no good reason at all. As it died, we were evicted from our home in a foreign country. With a newborn baby and a dog, thousands of miles from our family and friends.

We were left with nothing.

So how did it happen?

Good question.

We want to tell you about the creation of our little Croatian hotel. We want to tell you about the village that surrounded it, and the people who came into our lives in the three years we lived there. We want to tell you how we responded to the way we were treated. To this day, it still gives us and many of the locals a reason to smile.

Jonathan and I fell in love, and not long after, we fell in love with Croatia. We took the plunge, grabbed our dog Sailor, left California, and traveled 6,000 miles to live and work in the country in Eastern Europe.

We'd just turned thirty and left the States to breathe new life into a rundown old building halfway across the world. Our aim had been to create a beautiful boutique hotel from what was left of an old communist meeting house in the tiny village of Zaton.

We had our challenges from the day we arrived.

We were used to the sun and in our new home we found we were so cold we could watch our own breath when we laid in bed. We were design professionals, but found ourselves working with a construction crew who drank more during working hours than we could believe.

Since we only spoke English, we struggled to navigate conversations with people in a language that had seven different tenses!

On our journey we encountered Balkan landmines, faced officials who only worked for bribes, and were caught up in a huge criminal investigation that would see an entire squad of undercover police take up residence in our hotel.

We learned how to explain to family that amazingly enough, living through those events actually contributed to our greatest days in the most beautiful place on Earth. Yet, we found out how it felt when betrayal emptied your heart. When people you knew emptied your bank account.

As our world turned upside down, it felt like nothing would ever go our way again. Then our little boy arrived and changed everything. He came along just as we had started to forget ourselves, as we were struggling to see the beauty right in front of our eyes.

We called him Roko, after a saint greatly loved in Croatia, especially Zaton.

No matter what was wrong in every other part of our lives, Roko reminded us every day that everything we did was for love. Because this crazy Croatian story of ours is our family's love story, we dedicate it to him.

For Roko.

ONE

Croatia Journal: La Perla Hotel
October 2015.

THE first hotel we looked at had a big hole in the ceiling. The La Perla.

The room was spacious, and the view was great. The bathroom was fine too, even though the last makeover was, at a guess, 1985. The truth was the décor could bring on a headache. But we were looking beyond the cosmetics at the time, looking for potential, not problems.

Yet, seriously, that hole in the ceiling!

It's not that it would be a major problem to fix it, nor that it would be the main takeaway from that viewing. It was just weird no one had mentioned it.

Niko was one of three people who showed us around, tempting us to take on the whole place.

"Nice room," he said, nodding. "Yes?"

We nodded back, smiled, and agreed it sure was a nice room. But he had to know, right? About the hole? It was like... three feet across. There was even a ladder there that reached up to the hole from the floor and went right up into the room above.

Without a doubt, the oddest thing we'd ever seen in a hotel.

At least we knew we had both seen it. That hole. It wasn't some jetlagged induced figment of our imaginations. It looked like the ceiling had been smashed through with a hammer. Or like someone had fallen right through the floor above. Instead of fixing it, it's like someone got a ladder and said, "Hey look, here's a way guests can go from room to room. It cuts out all that crap known as opening doors."

Honestly, we were taking in the moment. We couldn't believe we were business partners, hotel browsers, and out to investigate what we might take on.

Also showing us the hotel was Niko's partner, Andrea. They made up the La Perla management team, and we assumed, the entire staff. Also there was Niko's father, Karlo, who owned the place.

We enjoyed meeting them all, especially Niko and Andrea. We'd been in touch for a while. Skyping, emailing. We'd talked about what might be a reasonable offer. We knew Karlo was keen to strike a deal either to sell the place or to take us on as tenants.

We played it cool, committed to nothing, and were waiting to see what the trip brought. Caution seemed appropriate. It's not like either of us had run a hotel in a former socialist republic before.

Niko and Andrea had a clear enthusiasm for the old place. It was obvious they could see the potential in that ex-communist meeting house. A sure and sturdy inn with the super pretty little horseshoe bay right out front.

They smiled a lot, expressed with open hands in a friendly Italian kind of way. Actually, where we were standing, there was nothing but 270 miles of water between us and Italy.

A lot of nodding and body language said this was all good. The body language was useful because there was a language barrier as big and obvious as that hole in the ceiling. Our Croatian, at this point, was as good as our skills in nuclear physics. Without Andrea, who had a good grasp of the English language, that tour would've just been people smiling and waving.

We took notes and jotted down our thoughts on paper as we walked around. The place was open for business, but as far as we could tell, didn't have any guests other than us. So this had been our chance to really get our eyes on every bit of the place.

The village of Zaton (with the Zat like in Cat) means bay or inlet in Croatian. It's home to a couple of hundred people, a little more than halfway down the coast. It's about a ten minute drive north from the old fortress town of Šibenik (pronounced She-bee-nik), and a little over an hour's drive north from Split (Split), the capital city of the Dalmatia region.

If you didn't know the area but Dalmatia rang a bell, it's perhaps because of those 101 spotty dogs. Their roots were in that region. As the story goes, Dalmatians were bred in the area to pull carts and chase down rats. But there's nothing to prove that's really true so you can believe whatever you like. The Disney stories are definitely not true, by the way.

We arrived in the little village of Zaton in darkness the night before and woke to catch the sunrise over the bay. Then we had breakfast with our four hosts and began to get our first glimpse of La Perla beyond the pictures. Those pictures, as the fact-finding trip revealed to us, didn't tell the full story.

We discovered a lot of the hotel was fragranced with the stench of cigarette smoke. A smell so strong it was like it had been pumped into the walls. We thought perhaps it was the leftover pong from decades of gatherings, parties, and political showdowns, during which everyone smoked as much as they could. That smell was clearly being faithfully topped up by Andrea and Niko, who lived in the hotel, and who both smoked like smoke grenades.

There was also a running theme of the falling apart guest wardrobes that were crammed with junk, which was cool as long as guests didn't want a place to put their clothes.

We noticed that the bedding was all mixed up as well. If there was a word for the theme, that word would be random. There was a lot of peachy yellow and wood paneling, which looked like ugly was covering up beauty. Plenty of fake Venetian plaster around too, which we assumed was meant to give the place a classic Italian look. It didn't.

There was way too much aging IKEA furniture and some of the bathrooms had ghoulish looking old black-spotted mirrors, which made users look like they had a fatal disease.

In every room was a tiny out of place rug, which, according to Andrea, had to be there because that was the law. Every room also had two small towels that seemed to be made from some kind of lightweight cardboard.

On the exterior wall of the hotel was a plaque to honor Marshal Tito, the President of formerly communist Yugoslavia, who died in 1980. As Americans in Croatia, we tried to be cautious and play it safe in these situations, so we smiled weakly when we saw the plaque.

Josip Broz Tito was called a 'benevolent dictator' by those who sympathized, but he invested in what are referred to as 'murder squads' by those who didn't share the sentiment. He basically killed people who disagreed with him. Joseph Stalin, who ruled the Union of Soviet Socialist Republics (USSR) until 1953, didn't like Tito much after he rejected his brand of hardline Russian communism for Yugoslavia.

So, as you might expect, there were claims that the Soviet Union's 'Man of Steel' tried to have Tito assassinated a few times.

Massively stubborn Tito survived them all and stayed in charge of his independent fiefdom and outlived Stalin by almost three decades.

A Serbian guy, Radoš Stevlić, also attempted to get rid of Tito, but that didn't work out either. Stevlić moved to America afterwards, and at Tito's request, got picked up by the FBI in the 1970s. Stevlić did ten years in an American jail and lived the rest of his life in Phoenix, Arizona, dying in 2016 of natural causes.

In the end, Tito, while in his eighties, suffered circulation problems but refused to have his left leg amputated to save his life.

By the time he had agreed to the chop, it was too late. He died from gangrene. Tito left a complicated legacy because, although he felt he had the right to have dissidents killed anywhere in the world, he was seen as a man who united a disparate region. And, he never feared Stalin, the most fearsome man of his era.

Until 1992, that region of Europe south of Austria and north of Greece was part of the 100,000 square mile bloc known as the Socialist Federal Republic of Yugoslavia. After Tito told Stalin to kiss his ass in the 1940s, it became its own unique thing. Yet, like the USSR, it did have the same kind of deal going on in terms of Americans being condemned as capitalist fools while the populace embraced Levi jeans and The Dukes of Hazzard.

Before making the move, we discussed what we might need to know about the USA's political relationship with Croatia. We found out that it's complicated, turbulent, and in many cases took a chunk of the lives of a lot of people there. We figured, in the end, we would be better off avoiding getting into it with the locals. Basically, we decided to read situations as they came up and to keep those smiles and frowns on standby.

Our families had touched on all that too, and pointed out Croatia had been involved in a four-year war of independence with neighboring Serbia since 1991. As communism fell and the Yugoslavian federation collapsed, its six republics jostled for position in a new era. Things turned bad, very bad, as ethnic tensions and independence struggles took hold. After the guns fell silent, more than 15,000 Croatians were dead and over 300,000 had been forced to leave their homes.

All of this was tragic, heavy-duty stuff. All of it was in the living memory of people even our own age. You could see why we didn't want to land there with any opinions on the situation other than that it was a tragedy.

Our response to the concerns of loved ones was that, because Croatia was a place emerging from its recent past, it was fertile ground for future-focused development. We said that tourism was on the rise and that Americans were starting to explore the place. The war was over anyway, and we could be part of the peace.

We couldn't say we won everyone over, but we were going anyway. In truth, we didn't let them know just how much we were set on the idea before we left on our fact-finding mission and didn't say just how determined we had become to do business out there. We knew as we left America that the next time they saw us we would probably be hoteliers. Truth was, we were already madly in love with Croatia. It's a thing that happens when people see it. It's an astonishing place.

Part of the mission that week was to get promotional material, photographs, and footage of some of the sights before the big white winter closed in. Our aim had been to view the handful of properties we had picked out online, talk with some suppliers, and work out some rough costs in terms of getting things started.

Truthfully, there was no time, not one single minute of that fifteen-hour flight from the USA to Zagreb, in which we did not think we might be out of our minds. But all the way along we were buoyed by the thrill of dramatic change. Energized by the thought of getting off our asses to make the break from our stuck-in-a-rut L.A. lives.

Before we went, we approached some video professionals from Salt Lake City about securing quality footage of Croatia. With perfect symmetry, they happened to be in Europe at the same time we were there and able to meet us. We'd worked hard putting together a preemptive package to sell Croatia as a destination back home. Our goal was to be back there and open for business by the summer of 2016.

Finding La Perla had been a challenge. We got a rental car at the airport and worked out the route. We needed to drive because we'd been planning a few days of trekking around to cover a good amount of ground. After getting lost for a while, we ended up on some backroads as we headed down the Adriatic coast into the Dalmatia region. After about three hours we began to zoom in on little Zaton. We arrived at La Perla, exhausted and hungry, around ten at night.

The night was warm and clear and the little fishing boats were bobbing around in the bay. Andrea and Niko were waiting at the door with open arms and big smiles. We wanted to apologize for taking so long, but they were apologizing first. Andrea was quickly saying she was sorry that half the streetlights in Zaton were out, that the hotel needed work, and that we might not find everything perfect. We told her we didn't want it to be perfect, we just wanted it to feel right. We knew she understood.

From there we had a few pastries to satisfy the hunger (there's no working kitchen in the hotel) and went up to our overnight room. Along the way we feasted our eyes on the peach plaster and filled our noses with a thousand flavors of old tobacco that lingered in the building. With the sound of the sweet little watery gurgles of a fishing harbor late at night, we crashed out hard.

We woke to see sunlight taking over our room. We took those few steps to the balcony and our hearts filled and took off like airships.

The little boats were sailing up the inlet and out to sea. The brilliant blue water carried them between the deep green slopes of either side. The gorgeous white and cozy homes of Zaton lined the bay. We took a moment to inhale deeply at the start of a day we'd been waiting for.

When we did, we realized the air, pretty unexpectedly, smelled a little like shit. Literally.

When we saw Andrea, we intended to bring up the issue of the bad smells inside and outside. Before we could, she started apologizing again. She said she was sorry about all the crap in the wardrobes and other places.

We laughed, said we noticed, and that it didn't matter. We were still laughing as we named what we could remember of the clutter. The rolls of cloth, tiles, metal rods, books, boxes of spare parts for who knows what; a fireguard, an old telephone, old pillows.

Andrea translated it all to her partners and whispered what we were saying about Niko's father's junk collection into Niko's ear. He laughed too.

She said Niko's dad, Karlo, who bought up property here and there, wouldn't let anything go just in case he found a use for it further down the line. We told them we were interested to know if he ever found a use for half a picture frame, a chair leg, or a rock. She laughed and said there was a lot more junk in the attic. We said we believed her and laughed some more.

We asked to see it. The attic, not the junk.

She and Niko took us back to one of the rooms. The one with the hole in the ceiling.

"That's the attic, do you see?" Andrea said. "Up the ladder and into the hole in the ceiling?"

We could see it.

(Megan)

JONATHAN and I got soaked on our last day in Croatia. We had stayed in Šibenik the night before. The streets of the old city were like rivers as we tried to get to our rental car. We parked on one of the really narrow lanes and had to turn around. Inch by inch, stop and start, reverse, then forward, as the water poured down. We'd never seen weather like that there. It really took us by surprise. The rainstorm didn't quit and was with us the entire four-hour drive to the airport.

We settled in at the airport and laughed about it, writing notes, and waiting for the flight home. We'd seen all we needed to see, toured the boutique hotels within our reach, and got some great footage and photography.

It'd been a good trip.

The night before, I'd read up on life in the country, looking at some unusual facts, nuggets of history.

While we waited at the airport, I turned to my boyfriend and said, "Hey, Jonathan. Serious conversation time."

"Okay," he said.

"Did you know you could've been arrested here for criticizing Marshal Tito when he was in charge?"

"I didn't know that."

"Yeah. He was into the whole, send-people-to-labor-camps thing, too. His secret police killed a lot of people to make him happy."

"Doesn't sound good."

"Did you know Croatia has 1,244 islands?" I asked.

"I actually did know that," he replied.

"Okay. So confession time."

"Okay."

"I've been thinking about the really pretty hotel? The one that didn't have a hole in the ceiling or the shit in the wardrobes."

"Oh yeah," he said. "I remember that one. The non-peach stucco one with actual beds that wasn't dedicated to a communist leader and didn't have a smokey stink inside or a shitty smell outside."

"That's the one. Let's not get it."

"I agree."

I told him it was weird that I already had so many plans for the hotel in little Zaton with the hole in the ceiling.

He laughed and said, "I do too. *La Perla*. Can't stop thinking about it. So much potential."

I said it felt right. That it had much to love about it. That
when we were there it felt like we were supposed to be there.

Jonathan agreed.

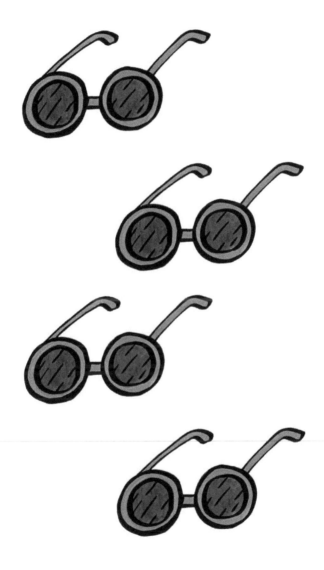

TWO

(Jonathan)

I was going to tell you about Megan, about that girl I met in 2015, I would tell you about the I5. It's the main north-south route in southern California that pretty much clings to the Pacific coast below L.A.

I would tell you that Megan drove that freeway up and down over and over from her job in Los Angeles as an interior designer to visit her parents. It's part of our story because it's down that road that we got together in the first place.

It can be a tough one to drive because it gets choked up with traffic, total bumper to bumper most days. It can be five mph or less when the weekenders are heading out of town or back into the city.

But Megan likes it for the view, and she can get great glimpses of the ocean now and then. She loves to see the big sparkling water meet the big blue sky.

I know that road well and we talked about it a few times after we met. About how it's iconic to many people in America. It's right on the edge of the country as far as you can go. We both love it when the sun slides behind the Pacific horizon, and pours out its red, amber, and yellow colors onto the land. It paints the traffic all around and pretties up the world beyond the windshield.

When Megan is on the I5 and the view of the sea is blocked by the kind of construction that has no business stealing all that glory, she pictures what she's missing. She likes to tear away concrete mountains in her mind and pretend to push them to the side so she gets to enjoy the kind of California she came there for in the first place.

You know what else she told me? Megan said that one time, only once, when she was stuck in her car on that road going nowhere, she got onto Tinder. She used the app because she was bored and sitting on the blacktop, doing nothing.

That's how we found each other.

Megan had been in California five or six years before we met, working hard, struggling sometimes, winning sometimes. But she was doing what she wanted to do: reimagining people's places, refreshing people's homes, making people's personal spaces happier, more liveable, more loveable. We're talking about one of the most competitive markets on the planet in terms of interior design, so she really had to prove herself.

She grew up in Jasper, Indiana, and went to school there. It's a city of about fifteen, maybe, twenty thousand people. She moved out to Arizona when her family relocated and began working in Scottsdale. She made a plan to move to L.A., aiming to make a name for herself.

Her folks moved around a little with work so perhaps it was serendipity that caused them to settle in San Diego, about 120 miles from Megan's little apartment in Santa Monica. The trip to her parents' house should take around two hours but when the I5 becomes a long, slow line of steel, it can take four, even five hours.

The day we first connected was one of the bad ones, in traffic terms. It was bottlenecking at the offramps and people were going nuts stuck in their cars.

Coming out to the edge of America had been a big step for her. But isn't it in the big steps when life really gets lived? The decision to go west was as much about the beach as anything else. Sure, it was in California where she could really start to climb the ladder, but she had thought about getting close to the coast for a long time and felt drawn to it. I guess if there's one thing Arizona and Indiana have in common, it's a lack of ocean.

She'd been working in Scottsdale when a company project in Malibu, a ritzy beach town about thirty minutes from L.A., came along. It was a perfect fit, a no-brainer. It wasn't anything huge, but it would keep her there for a couple of months. So she told colleagues she was going for it.

She told them that, when it was done, she wouldn't be coming back. That she wanted to make L.A. home at least for a while. She arrived knowing she had a couple of months of work ahead of her, but the rest was unknown.

Megan was pretty confident she would succeed.

Turned out that a few old friends from the Midwest were in the area too. Others who wanted to make a go of it in L.A. and liked to kick back by the ocean when they could. They would get together and keep each other grounded in a place that can definitely overwhelm and chew you up fast if you didn't pay attention.

Those were great times. Four Hoosiers in a little Santa Monica house just ten minutes from the beach. Four girls finding fun in a new lifestyle. I know they had fun laughing at some of the California surfer dude types and the city slicker wannabe pick up artists.

Megan went to work for *Adam Hunter Inc*, which was absolutely one of the best interior design firms in L.A. That was a great chance to really knuckle down and prove herself some more. By the time we met, she was a tried, tested, and trusted senior designer. She worked on high-end projects with influential and celebrity clients and with people able to really buy into big ideas.

There's that side to her, the aiming high and fighting hard side, compelled to create beautiful things. Then there's that young woman on the I5, trapped in her car, and just wanting to get the wheels rolling. Tearing down buildings in her mind as she played at improving the scenery blocked by construction and ruined by traffic congestion.

I found out pretty quickly Megan likes to keep moving in her life. Megan didn't plan to live in California forever. For her, it was always some kind of a stepping stone on the path of her life, and those itchy feet which brought her to L.A. were the same ones that would move her somewhere else sooner or later. She'd been thinking how she felt closed in at times, and the balance of location, career, opportunity and quality of life had all gotten repositioned.

The cost of everything in LA had gotten so crazy as well, almost out-of-control. She spent too much time making decisions about what to sacrifice, what to save. That was an incentive for her to find another way of achieving things. Find another place to achieve them.

I agreed with a lot of what she said. I definitely knew what she meant when she said a lot of the guys could be dicks. She talked about the ones who took that Cali surfer dude thing way too seriously, who live it for way too long. I had lived some of that life and agreed they could be dicks.

On the day we connected, in the summer of 2015, she was in her little car on that big road, I5, inching her way through Orange County, on her phone, checking out Tinder, swiping left, left, left. She was having fun, shaking her head at the guys online, feeling maybe a little cynical about it all.

She'd come to a full stop in her car and was focused on the view you get out that way. The space and the light right before the City surrounds it. She said that right before we connected, she was drumming her fingers and waiting to move.

(Megan)

THE first thing I knew about Jonathan was that he was from Orange County. That's one of the reasons Tinder matched us together. I was on I5 when Tinder flagged him for me.

I could tell right away he was a guy who understood images, and that he was a visually creative person. In fact, if you knew Jonathan, you'd know he takes his camera everywhere and takes a lot of pictures. Photography is part of who he is.

With Jonathan, it's both a serious addiction and genuine talent. And what's so good about that is that it keeps him exploring, keeps his eyes wide and looking for vivid things, for patterns, arrangements, color, character, and adventure.

His dog's name is Sailor, a Hungarian Vizsla. She was in the Tinder picture that first caught my eye and was in Jonathan's viewfinder on that same day. He'd been taking those shots of her in sharp focus with the azure Pacific in the background. Sailor has a golden rust coat and I remember Jonathan saying she adds an easy fierceness to every image he shoots with her. That she delivered a new, natural tone to his output.

Jonathan's pictures really brought out the beauty of Sailor, in the way his photographs always brought you right to the beauty of things. Right away, I wanted to know more about how he saw things.

After we met, I talked about those pictures of Sailor, about how so many people commented about them online. People said the images looked good and that Sailor was like a wild copper splash surrounded by the yellows and blues of the coast. She was so cool and getting locally famous because of the pictures. She'd been in shots with friends of his, with relatives, with strangers.

One of Jonathan's best pictures with her was like a selfie. One he arranged for his mom. It was a recreation of a childhood photo, him lying on his stomach, hands under the chin, feet kicking around in the air and little Sailor alongside. He liked that his mom put that one on the wall.

Sailor was graceful in those shots but is otherwise basically insane, even for a dog. It's so funny to see Jonathan trying to reason with her about the inappropriateness of getting the zoomies on Laguna Beach when she should really be on a leash. He was always trying out dog psychology tricks to get the upper hand, but if you knew Sailor, as I do now, you'd know she's too smart for that.

She had him running around and shouting out, *"Sailor, no, no, NOOOOO!"* Among all the tourists so many times. I've seen him look her in the eye and try to explain how better behaved she is when off-leash and the better it is for both of them. It's a total waste of time but it's kinda cute. Anyway, it's obvious he prefers it when Sailor's free to explore her world even if others sometimes don't like it.

On that day we made contact, Jonathan was taking some shots, but had to get back to work for a prearranged overseas call. He worked during the day in a beachfront store selling preppy surf wear. The store was *Latitude Supply Company*. He owned the business and was the creative director adding his flair to men and women's gear. He wasn't looking forward to the call.

It was some business matter, a query around the shipping details of some shirts he had sent from A to B. So many of the calls he took at the time were about those kinds of details, about process not product. Another week of the same grind was just beginning for him, where he would again have to find all the hours to make sure every link in the manufacture, dispatch, and delivery chain was holding strong.

Things had really taken off for Jonathan's business online and that was the nature of most of his work at that point. Bigger firms were buying into what he was creating, and the paperwork was taking over.

That was the irony of Jonathan at that time. He'd done really well and knew he should've been more excited about his success. But the outworking of it were getting more and more complicated, frustrating, and overwhelming. He told me how it had been annoying him, and he couldn't escape the truth that he wasn't enjoying it as much as he once did.

His stuff had a lot of nautical styling in it, inspired by a childhood by the sea. The tones and shades and spirit were artistic responses to those years with sand under his feet and saltwater on his skin.

Jonathan was west coast raised by east coast parents and the family crisscrossed the USA many times. Jonathan talked easily about how different places were in different seasons, about variations in forms and functionality of clothing, culture, buildings, and cityscapes over many miles.

What he made at the time – T-shirts, swimwear, blazers, everything was made to work with the lifestyle of the west coast, not to dictate what it should be. That's how I saw it. His goal had been to hit somewhere close to midpoint between the standout east and west themes. That seemed to make good sense, given his background.

His progression had been awesome. He started designing in school, graphic T-shirts and all of that, and really made something of it fast. From there he moved into clean-cut signature shapes and began to push it all onto that line between preppy and surfie.

Eventually I saw every design he ever came up with and I'm biased, but it was undeniably fresh, spirited, upbeat stuff. And that's why it was taking off so well. It hit the spot when people went looking for original American cuts and concepts.

Yet the other side was that the business customers, ironically, were sucking the fun out of it all. Jonathan found himself working at bulk level and under pressure to produce clothes a year in advance so he could hit the right market. All ultimately a gamble in a totally saturated clothing market where everything fed off everything else.

Online was where the volume was and where the money was being made. Where the whole thing made commercial sense and he wasn't going to shy away from giving it all a shot. But the business-to-business way of working was also where the links in the chain broke the easiest and the losses hit the hardest.

Jonathan had a couple of major clients in Asia and honestly, it was a nightmare to get the timing right, to strike the right deals. It was an inexact, colorless business science that could finish him financially in a heartbeat. It kept him awake at night when all he wanted to do was design and create. It made him question how much of himself he wanted to give to all of it.

The first international order he ever placed for manufacturers was ambitious. That's how fast things moved. He had to upscale production in a short time and needed to get thousands of bathing suits, button-up shirts, pants, shirts, tank tops put together quickly. I think he celebrated signing off on that like it was the realization of a dream. But all of it got held up in customs in L.A. so he missed a bunch of shipping slots which led to a string of cancellations and a huge loss of money and heart.

It had been a whole pile of bullshit over which, once he pressed click, he had zero control. I was sad to hear about it because I knew he deserved better and it was probably a turning point in his mind. It didn't get any less messy after that. His mind drifted further and further from his work, back to a dream he had when he was in his teenage years.

The phone call Jonathan had to take on the day we connected was about that, about an order, about dates, times, packaging, about price per unit. It was about penalties if it went wrong, about buy back options, about problems, problems, problems. It was all passionless, pain in the ass stuff when he was told at the end how there were a thousand other Americans the client could approach.

Jonathan, at that moment when I reached out to him for the first time, probably had the phone at his ear, was looking at his camera, looking out at the sea, over at Sailor, and not giving a shit about that call.

I know that because when the call ended, he grabbed the leash, the camera and his phone. As he was headed out, that's when he heard the tri-tone, Tinder message sound.

And a hello.

From me.

Megan.

Stuck on the I5, sending him a message.

I wrote, *Hi. I like the goofy picture of you with your dog.*

THREE

Croatia Journal: Zaton, Dalmatia.
January 2016.

Thanks to things like climate, geography, and Sailor's attitude, it took us a week to get back to Croatia, once we were committed. After we knew *La Perla* was the one for us, we got back to L.A. and went to work fast. One of the first things we did was set up a crowdfunding account to invite people to invest in what we were planning to do.

The trip back was not uneventful. Sailor needed more drugs than Charlie Sheen to calm her down before she'd get on the plane. At the same time, if she's off-her-dogface, she's considered 'too high to fly' and they wouldn't take her. It had been a puzzle trying to get that balance right. Weird having people look in her eyes to see how buzzed she was.

We had much to learn. And not just about Sailor's narcotics tolerance. When we got back to Croatia, it took a week or more to get our bearings. To get a better sense of what was around us beyond the water that immediately won so much of our attention.

One of those complications was that we found minefields.

Literally.

You knew them by the red triangle with the skull and crossbones, the international symbol for minefields. At least we figured it out fairly quickly. We had no idea we were moving to a mine zone. It never came up before we arrived. When we saw the first sign we figured it wasn't good. Skulls and crossbones usually aren't.

The sign read, *Ne prilazite na ovom podrucju je velika opasnost od mina*. Rough translation, *Keep away - landmines*.

We got the message.

The mines were left over from the Croatian War of Independence. The more tourist friendly vernacular, mine suspected areas, were thought to still contain some 20,000 landmines and covered more than a hundred square miles of the country.

Without meaning to seem in any way alarmed, we asked our new, and entire workforce, Niko and Andrea, about the landmine situation. They were in their early twenties and too young to remember the conflict but we wondered what they knew nevertheless.

Were there really armed bombs hidden all over the fields and hills of the area that we had just moved to with our dog, or was this more a precautionary thing? We wanted to know if we had relocated to what could be described as some form of live battlefield even though the war was long over. It felt like a fair question.

"Yes, yes, sorry," Andrea said, needlessly apologizing once again. "Go only on the paths to keep away from the mines."

This news wasn't at the top of the list of things we were going to tell the folks back home, especially not the handful of investors who had bought into what we pitched about this being an oasis of peace on the Dalmatian coast. We had a short meeting in which we decided to keep the bomb issue on the down low for a while.

Andrea said we would occasionally see teams of mine clearing people around. These were some seriously brave people from the *Croatian Mine Action Centre*. They worked every day to clear those devices out of the way step by cautious step, scanning the ground and surgically removing them. Andrea said their job would be finished in a while. We checked out what 'a while' was, and it turned out, it was about ten years.

Mine clearing wasn't exactly the sort of work that could be rushed. Sixty or more deminers had been killed while trying to make the place safer. It was dangerous work. They should take as long as they needed.

We thanked Andrea and followed up with a question probably best posed to someone with experience in placing mines. We asked, "Do you think a dog could trigger a landmine?"

She didn't know. No one really knew and we didn't really know who else to ask.

We suspected Sailor might be okay. We discussed it in another brief management meeting. At three-years-old, Sailor was very fast when dashing around, but she was lightweight too. Would she be below the weight that triggered one of those things?

It's a shitty situation, across huge parts of the region. Andrea and Niko were able to tell us what their parents had told them about the relatively recent past, and some of it shocked us. A couple million mines, give or take, were laid by battling Serbs and Croats during the War of Independence and most never went off. It was definitely good that all those bombs didn't get to do what they were designed to do, but not so good that they had no set period when they became inert.

Of the many things that were on our minds when we first took on the hotel, losing our lives to a war that ended a couple of decades back was not among them. Also, we hadn't factored the landmine issue into the experience we were trying to market.

So, we decided we would tactfully advise our first guests, who we were expecting in four month's time, about the issue when they arrived.

It all felt real. We'd made the move, unpacked our dog and stuff, and knew we had so much to get to grips with and so much to do.

Our vision for the hotel was online for a while on social media and had been updated to say work was about to begin. We'd been pushing pretty hard for months, talking up our plans, showing some of the footage of the not-too-shabby *Krka National Park* in the region, showing off some of the islands off the coast, showing some of the village itself.

In all that time we'd been reworking the La *Perla* hotel in our heads, focusing on our best ideas, mapping out what was needed to make the dreams come alive. We put together renderings that really captured something about where we were from and who we were and fused it all with the flawless location of the hotel. To that point, things were good with all the fusing.

What wasn't so good was we did not at that stage have anything in any way reassuring from a single tradesman in terms of helping us with the mammoth task ahead. We figured we would cross that bridge when we came to it, and we could definitely see the bridge right in front of us.

If there was a way to sum up how we were rolling at that particular time, it's probably just lots of very short meetings. We knew it'd be a challenge before we arrived, of course, but we also knew before arrival that we were capable, adaptive, resourceful people. But somehow it was like we were standing on the stage before the audience had arrived, that they were being promised a great show, and we were looking at each other saying, "How in the hell are we going to do this?"

(Megan)

Before we made the move, Jonathan and Sailor were already living in my very small apartment in Santa Monica. It was one street off Lincoln Boulevard, a cozy one bedroom first-floor unit. I had definitely been comfortable there but did have a weird feeling that something in my life was going to change right before it did. I hadn't expected the change to be that a man and dog would move in.

I wanted to make sure they felt as comfortable as possible, to make them feel as if it was their home. So, I took some paintings down, let Jonathan choose some pictures to put up, things like that. We worked with Sailor to make sure she was happy, so she knew where her food would be, where to sleep, and everything was good.

I have to say she liked a lot of contact and was pretty keen to sleep on the bed with us at first. I had to work on that a little, and had to try a few persuasion techniques on both Sailor and Jonathan because I was the only one who raised this as an issue. I mean, seriously, it was not a big apartment.

A little space here and there, please.

The rules said we weren't allowed pets but I knew Jonathan and Sailor were a package deal and I had bonded well with her by that time anyway. So, we wargamed out a little bit of smuggling, a stealthy operation getting her in and out, and we figured we would be able to do it.

It was great in the mornings for us to get up together, to sneak our sweet red puppy outside, to run to the beach and back.

One of the great things was that suddenly I had better food in my life because Jonathan's a really good chef. He had some signature dishes so sometimes I would get home and he would have prepared something pretty substantial, like the Irish lamb dish he picked up from his mom.

In the evenings, we did a lot of research into the Croatian economy and Dalmatian tourism in particular. We searched out other boutique hotels offering something close to the kind of experience we hoped to offer, generally compiling a business plan. We designed a brochure about our hotel and began to reach out to potential investors.

Jonathan launched the crowdfunding website to get an even wider reach, to show off the pictures and video we had captured around Zaton, the bay, the boats, the islands, *Krka National Park*, Šibenik.

What was playing on my mind was that I would have to break away from the job I loved at *Adam Hunter Inc*. That involved breaking away from Adam himself, a brilliantly talented boss who had come to mean so much to me. Adam was one hundred percent my gay husband.

When it came time to tell him I had to go, the tears came. I was saying goodbye to someone who'd been so much more than an employer. He'd been the kindest, funniest, and most thoughtful working companion, the closest and most dependable friend, and an invaluable influence on my personal and professional life.

He paid me the most generous compliment there was when he placed his complete trust in me. I just loved my time working with him and I'll always be in his debt. The day I told him I had to go was one of the most difficult days of my life. What lay ahead for Jonathan and I was exciting, but it hurt to get it done.

Jonathan had to wrap things up with *Latitude Supply Co* and he wasn't too upset about that. He had let the store go by that time and had an office studio in downtown LA. It had been beating him down a little because he's not a great guy for paperwork and detail. And anyway, a new adventure lay ahead. But I was sad to see him step away from his own company, to see him let it fall. He had worked hard to build it to what it was.

So, within a month of getting back from Croatia on our fact-finder mission we went live with our vision. We went on Facebook and Instagram and announced to the world, although we also admitted we hadn't quite made up our minds yet, that *La Perla* would become *The Admiral*.

And, oh God, there were a lot of questions from everyone.

"So, you have renamed this place *The Admiral* and made plans for how it's going to look even though you're not a hundred percent sure you're going?"

"Yeah," we would say. "We're just thinking things through, taking the temperature."

"You are advertising to the world that you're opening a business in the middle of Croatia in a few months but it's not a done deal?"

"That's right."

"Isn't there a war there?"

We got asked that a lot. "No, it's over."

"Do you speak any Croatian?"

"Not a word."

"You're really going, aren't you?"

"We think so."

"Have you lost your minds?"

"We don't think so."

"Have you guys run a hotel before?"

"What's that now? Not exactly. But we've got experience in... look, how hard can it be?"

"What if you go ahead and do it but you break up when you're out there. You two haven't even been together for a year!"

"Yeah, we're thinking more positively than that."

The breakup end of things wasn't something we had discussed. Should we have thought about how we might start to hate each other? No need. There was no suggestion at all between us that this relationship was in any way fragile or temporary. We both felt like we had clicked into some kind of building mode. And what we were building would be our whole lives.

We would say to people, "What do you think of the pictures of Croatia?"

"Stunning."

"That national park is something, don't you think?"

"Amazing."

"Ten percent of the whole country is parkland and reserves. Isn't that cool?"

"That is cool."

"Wouldn't it be cool to run a little hotel in a place like that, at least for a while?"

"Sure," our friends would say.

"You know, it's relatively inexpensive out there to do business."

"Is it?"

And we would say, "Did you know there are like 1,244 islands along the Dalmatian waterfront?"

"We didn't."

"That *Game of Thrones* used to be filmed there?"

"That's a new one to us."

"Did you know Croatia gets more sunshine than Sydney?"

"Nope."

"That the necktie was invented by Croatian soldiers?"

"Is that important?"

"Not really, but you get the point, right? We're basically smitten with Croatia and sometimes you have to just follow your heart."

"Okay, cool. So, you're definitely going?"

"We're not totally sure yet, but yes."

(Jonathan)

FOR Megan and me, it was like the east had become the new west, full of promise and adventure. Croatia had been emerging for years yet we still saw it as a place where those who think big and work hard could really create something lasting and special.

For us, it was like every inch of California, of America, was maxed out in terms of its potential. Croatia seemed like fresh, fertile ground, somewhere that touched our hearts and where the American Dream could be reimagined in a country turning its face to the future.

When we had any doubts, we would just cozy up together in our little L.A. apartment with our secret dog and remind each other of these things. It was a big gamble we were taking, we would say. But we were doing this for us and no one else. It didn't have to feel right for anyone but us.

Right at that point, we still had no watertight deal with Karlo, the owner of the hotel. We had seen the books on the factfinder, in terms of working out if it was really worth the money he wanted for the place, and we decided (quickly) that it wasn't.

La Perla wasn't working for him. We didn't want to show up waving dollars and buy a problem at an extortionate price. Instead, over time, we struck up a deal to lease the hotel for three years, to take control of everything inside – including the workforce of Niko and Andrea – and to remodel and market it as we saw fit.

Besides, we just didn't have the €1.5 million {$1,800,000} he wanted for the hotel. What we did have was the belief we could absolutely maximize its potential, fill its rooms every night of every season, and put it on the road to turning a profit. When all that was in play, our plan was to go back to Karlo and happily take the busy little hotel off his hands once and for all.

So with our deal almost flushed out, and with our plans drawn up, with the crowdfunding in play, we rolled up our lingual sleeves and said it was time to get stuck in. We wanted to arrive at least knowing how to read a sign, to be able to say *Hello* and *Please* and *Thank you* and *Do you speak English?*

That hadn't gone so well. We did try but really fell at the first hurdle. We figured it would be difficult, even more complex than French or Italian or German, but turned out it was so difficult, almost no one had even written a book about it.

We tried a few shops in L.A., looked online, but the options were seriously limited. We got an unimpressive little app, bought a few history books, some stuff about the culture of the place which we needed anyway, and a phrasebook that pretty much terrified us. In terms of the language for absolute beginners, this hadn't started well.

At one point Megan and I were basically reading about the Ottoman Empire's grip on chunks of Croatia in the 17th Century. We read aloud place names of the era, looking at each other to check if that might sound right.

But who were we kidding? There was nothing instinctive about what sounded right when it came to a language with seven or eight tenses and words with nine consonants and a vowel.

In the meantime, the crowdfunding never got off the ground. It ran for forty-five days and sank. I guess we were one of the first hotel concepts to give that platform a try. It was a bit of a mismatch. We got some minor publicity out of it, some interest in the idea, the high-quality visuals, and that was great. But none of that enthusiasm translated into dollars. Even if it had worked, in all honesty, it would have been a drop in the ocean.

Truth was the crowdfunding failure had hurt a little, even felt like a reality check for two people who, as some were suggesting, had lost track of reality. But we'd reached a point where a catastrophic lack of funding wasn't going to stop us.

Instead, we mopped up all we could of our own resources. We went through our detailed plans with friends and family, and friends-of-friends and friends-of-family. We let our ambition loose as we spoke to them all and did everything-we could to prove that what we had there was a golden opportunity for an off-beat investment.

We pitched that it would help enhance a little village that could do with a break and that we were getting involved in something that we were sure was going to work. We said it would give everyone a little getaway option on a European coastline that could not be more astonishing.

We made some good progress, but the truth remained that we didn't know how much we needed to remodel a hotel. How long would it be until we began making money? Much like in the way some people had been suggesting, we had very little idea what we were doing at all.

Megan left her job and that was tough for her. It was an emotional Christmas time, a few weeks living with a blend of excitement and sadness and fear and intense joy.

For my part, I closed the door on my business. I mean, just literally closed the door. I tried to shift some stock but it was halfhearted, to be honest. I put some in storage, sold off what I could, then just gave up, and closed the door. I knew I might live to regret that.

I had options and could have done things differently, but that was the way it was playing out and, I had to say, I'd never felt as passionate about any project as I did about this Croatian adventure.

The fact remained that it had all been a big and ongoing leap into the dark, jumping right out of at least some security and into the unknown. It was, *Goodbye employment. Goodbye comfort zone. Hello we-have-no-real-idea*.

We left organizing the journey pretty much until the eleventh hour, and for the record, that was mostly my fault. We had to get Sailor checked over by a vet in L.A., certified by the FDA in the US, just like you would when exporting a piece of meat.

Then it was a matter of figuring out which airline would take her that would get us closest to where we needed to be. That wasn't as simple as we thought it would be. We needed to fly out early to begin our work before the tourists arrived, so we chose January. And flying with animals in the already cold aircraft hold, in one of the coldest months of the year, as airlines advised us, can be the kind of gamble you don't want to take. So, it turned out, in terms of being safe, we could only get as far as Paris with her.

She was pretty stressed out about all the flights and didn't want to get into her box. She didn't like the airport, the people in the airport, the idea that her beloved owners had decided to send her to some kind of tiny jail. She was an outside dog all the way and that box concept was not for her.

So out came the drugs but not too much, and not too little. We found the sweet spot where she was balanced somewhere between calm and sleepy and they checked her over to see that she was okay. She definitely needed a little more than we had expected. What we did know was that Sailor was *higher* than she'd ever been before.

We went from L.A. to New York to Paris where it turned out she was just as unhappy with trains as she was with planes. So, we had to drug her again. Just a little this time. It worked, thankfully, but the downside of all the doping was that she kept relaxing her bladder. We got peed on a few times on the way there.

We rented a car for two days in Milan, drove all the way to Venice and dropped down into Croatia.

(Megan)

JONATHAN'S a nervous flyer. Sailor's a little worse. Me? No problem. Put me on any moving vehicle and I fall asleep. Another difference was that, ahead of travel, I'm more organized. Jonathan didn't even pack until the day before we left, which was frustrating.

Eventually, we got it all done, had bags everywhere, including a hundred pounds of camera equipment. The first flight was to JFK, New York, and already, without even leaving the USA, all but one of our bags was lost.

And then Jonathan lost his cellphone.

And then the JFK cargo guy said to us, "Dog? There was no dog on that flight."

After about thirty minutes, they located Sailor going crazy in her box. And then someone located Jonathan's cellphone. Given all the travel on trains, planes, and automobiles ahead of us, it was a blessing in disguise that they lost some of the luggage and said they would send it on.

We arrived in Zaton as all the people of the village were holding a funeral. The man who ran *Porat*, the little café right next door to *La Perla,* had just passed away. The very first thing we witnessed were people walking down the street towards the sea in somber unison, the widow in all black. We showed up on a downbeat note in a village that seemed to be coming together because its heart had broken. It felt like we'd landed on someone's grief.

It'd been a sad time for this little place. And it's freezing there too. And the heaters in the hotel barely worked. We noticed how there were heating units only in the walls in the hallway. But the bedrooms were ice cold. And the wind outside came charging down the inlet and felt like it could cut your ears off when it hit.

We picked a room, snuggled up, and talked about it all getting real now. We discussed following up with contractors we had approached. The people we really needed to help make all this work.

We'd gotten all cozy and talked about not focusing on that little old issue about us having limited funds. Or how we barely spoke a word of Croatian. Or that we thought Sailor was still stoned. Or that we were surrounded by landmines. Or that we had never felt as suddenly out of our-depth in our lives.

FOUR

(Jonathan)

When I was a little boy, I nearly drowned. So you could say it's weird that I love the water so much. But water was one of the reasons I loved Zaton. *La Perla* was just seconds from it. Water was one of the reasons I fell in love with Croatia in the first place. That happened in 2006, a whole ten years before I moved there.

You could leave *La Perla,* cross the road outside, and be right there. The village sits at the end of the long stretch of water cutting a channel into the land from the south, forming a glowing crystal blue basin. It runs parallel to the coast, almost to the doorstep of the hotel. There's a little old church in the small plaza beside it called the *Church of St Roko*. There are pretty little homes and cafes and offices and stores around there too, all on the cove just beyond the village. It all looks and feels right away like a place that's nothing other than happy.

Within a thirty-minute boat trip you can find fifty or more little islands, every one of them totally charming, many with a bar or restaurant, some with a tiny little village. No one could arrange beauty any better. I couldn't help but take picture after picture. Right away I was thinking about boat tours for guests, about taking Sailor on board, and of spending days gliding around randomly island hopping. The whole area was at one time the vacation hotspot for the wealthy families of Zagreb and if you spent a minute there you'd never need to ask why.

So, for me, that little bay at Zaton had *perfect* written all over it. I love being close to water, in water, on water. If I think of peace and happiness, I think about being around water.

But, as I said, at the start of my life, at age one, only a baby, it was nearly all over for me. I fell into the water and was declared dead at the scene. It freaked everyone out.

My parents were still married at the time and had this great house in Huntington Beach in Orange County. It was right on the harbor and had a boat docked beside it. There was a swimming pool at the house and, on that day, I was crawling and stumbling around in the grass, exploring the world. There was a ball somewhere. My ten-year-old sister had been throwing and bouncing it around and it ended up in the pool. Somehow I made my way over and put myself right in.

She saved me. My sister, Sara, saved my life. She jumped in and pulled me out of the water. The problem was I had already been in for a while and wasn't responsive. So there was a big drama at the side of the pool and I was given the kiss of life to get my baby lungs going again.

But they say things were pretty bleak.

A helicopter came along with paramedics. They said at first I was dead, that my heart had quit, but thankfully they kept on working on me. In the end they flew me to the hospital and it worked out okay.

But it had been traumatic for everyone, including the nanny who was supposed to have been watching me. I'm sorry about that. All my life I've had what sometimes feels like a kind of residual ironic response to what happened that day. I'm happiest in water, at my absolute most calm under the surface of what didn't get to kill me on that day.

I can get driven totally crazy by the ways of the world, and when that happens I honestly just need to dive in, salt or fresh, and I feel better. Or I can just get on a boat and get right out there away from the shore and fix myself. It's like therapy.

The theme running through my clothing designs was strongly nautical. The inspiration behind almost everything I've ever created goes right back to water. I'm just drawn to the way form and function meet in terms of mankind's way of interacting with the sea.

I've been way too excited about ideas of anchors, portholes, docks, boats, sea blues, horizons, waves, fish, all that can be found as you leave land. I mean, even my dog's called Sailor. I'm *Captain Steezy* on social media and the profile pic is of a sailor smoking a pipe (the creation of an artist friend).

When Megan and I opened a hotel right beside the water, we changed its name from *La Perla* to *The Admiral*.

So, do you believe in fate? Maybe not. Maybe you do. It doesn't matter. It's not really my thing. But you know... it's tempting sometimes, just the way the events of our lives have all fit together.

Megan and I have talked about how fate set out to get us together as a couple. We were in the same city in Arizona for three years when I was at college, and she was an intern. But fate missed its shot.

It's fun to imagine that fate dusted itself off and made up its mind to keep on going. Eventually, all the stars aligned, finally connected us, and sent Megan, Sailor, and I to Croatia, right into adventure's arms.

And then, as we were working with it like little playthings, it delivered the final part of its plan – to mercilessly crush our dreams and laugh in our faces. If fate's really out there, it's got one hell of a sense of humor. But it gave us some great times and it let us have the last laugh too. Maybe, in the end, fate is fair-minded.

In 2006, my older brother Brian and I went off the beaten track on a European backpacking trip, making our way down the Croatian coast. I was eighteen, a freshman in college, and had no real interest in the country. No real clue where it was, no real clue about much at all.

I'd been to Europe before but not eastern Europe. My brother was more mature and more interested in the world around him. He had planned the whole trip and he tried to make sure it was going to be something memorable.

He's a doctor and was in med school at the time. A lot of his friends had moved on while he was still studying and training. He came to me before that summer and said he really needed a change of scenery. He wanted to go to Europe and asked if I would come.

I said, "Sure."

So, he told me all about it. Paris, Rome, all of that, and I said, "Fine."

Then he mentioned a place called Croatia and I was like, "Okay, whatever."

He'd been reading about how it wasn't on the main tourist trail for Americans. That it was across from Italy on the other side of the Adriatic.

Brian said it was hot as hell in summer, cold as hell in the winter. It had been under one-party communist rule, just like Russia, all through the Cold War. He said it was an emerging nation now, pretty much virgin territory for travelers like us and that it was really worth a look.

And you know, he was right. It turned out to be something that caught hold of me and never let go. Not many things do that when you're eighteen.

I mean it in the nicest way possible when I say it was like there was nothing happening in Croatia at the time. We had come from the teeming streets and shores of America, typical backpackers in Europe. We wandered around some of the busiest cities in the world, with maps and cameras and beer, doing what many other Americans our age liked to do.

And we came to this place Croatia. It was like stepping back in time, culturally, socially, economically. It was like a quiet, unspoiled world, as if half the country was taking a nap.

The trip took us a couple of hundred miles down the west coast, the only coast. We stopped off in random fishing villages and found ourselves in little old bars and cafes where everyone was very sweet and no one spoke English.

We took an old bus to someplace with a name we couldn't pronounce and there was a little lady who looked like she was a hundred year's old sitting there with a hand-written cardboard sign saying *Apartment For Rent.*

We agreed to rent the room. She introduced us to her relatives and told us, in a mix of hand signals and in the heavy melody of the Croatian lingo, that we must drink home-made rakija. We were always well-mannered enough to know we should accept.

By the way, home-made rakija, the national drink, is a mysterious alcoholic beverage. It's like a fruit concoction with no one standard recipe, not even a standard fruit that gets passed down through generations like a precious heirloom. It often tastes like straight gasoline.

So that we would get a sense of the area, we had a full-flavored glass or two of that crazy kind of brandy in every place we went, and enjoyed the gentle implosion of our senses that day as the sun went down. We usually stayed in one place for just a night, paid a few kunas, and moved on to the next place. We would maybe meet another little babushka and enjoy another glass of fermented guess-the-fruit.

In the peaceful part of the trip, I noticed quietness, sometimes complete silence. And I marveled at those beautiful little harbors and perfect little bays and fishing boats bobbing around. There were amazing old cars from the Yugoslavia era, and the practical charm in the imposing postwar architecture.

There were old men everywhere we went. Guys who would get up in the morning and walk outside to meet their friends. They would always take a box and sit on them all day. Rotate with the sun as the hours flew by and discuss their world or else just stare into the distance.

My brother and I wondered how many of those old guys were still spiritually tied to the old communist calendar. Where the drive of industry and competition in the marketplace was something alien to them. We figured that bringing in a few kunas took a back seat to meeting your friends and sitting your butt on a box for eight hours. The poverty we saw was material but that Croatia's social culture and fabric were as rich as you could get anywhere.

You could say I was a cranky, bratty kid at the time. Probably the last person anyone more mature wanted to take backpacking. Yet some part of me got right into the rhythm of it all. Some piece of me absorbed that natural calm and beauty. The simplicity of it all. I saw it, heard it, and felt it. Really appreciating something that, on paper, would've had zero appeal to most people.

I never forgot those days or that place. I'd gone on many vacations and had many little breaks here and there over the years with my family. We'd been to Mexico, Hawaii, Jamaica, Israel, and France. My dad was always a big traveler and I loved to get away too. But this was different. People talk about finding places where you can escape from it all and, for me, Croatia in 2006 was that place. I guess it gave me a little personal break from my grumpy eighteen-year-old self. I grew up a little when I was there.

During my senior year, as part of my Tourism Development and Management degree at Arizona State, I had to write a thesis on setting up a business. I knew from the start that I would write about Croatia. I had it in my head that I would like to put together a paper on opening a hotel. I felt I could really put some passion into it and that I would enjoy researching the market and the country that had stayed with me since I had left there.

I didn't have any idea at that time that the girl I would fall in love with was also living in Scottsdale. I couldn't have known that in a few short years we would be running a boutique hotel in Croatia together.

Megan and I knew some of the same bars, some of the same places to hang out. Maybe we were in the same place some time when I was working on my thesis. Who knows? But it's nice to let the mind roll those things around once in a while.

Later as Megan and I got to know each other and understand what made each other tick, Croatia began to appear in our conversations. I mentioned it when we talked of color and design and seascapes and everything that was built around us. It came up sometimes when we talked about congestion, about how L.A. could eat up hours and resources and patience and sanity and life.

She knew I liked to get dreamy about what had taken my breath away a decade before. That it rose out of some happy place in my heart. Croatia took its cue to reemerge right as I was really falling for the girl who landed into my life from the I5.

I liked from the start that Megan was from small town Indiana. In my mind, there was something wholesome about that. It was novel for both of us that we had come from different parts of the country. I loved from the get go, that she was a designer, and that we were able to meet each other mentally on that visual level. We knew we weren't boring each other when we talked about things that fired us up.

So I told her that Croatia had really gotten under my skin and that I hoped it hadn't changed too much since I left as a tourist in 2006. I suggested we go there on vacation for my 28th birthday because I was sure she would love it too.

And we did go, and she did love it, and by the end of that trip I knew I wanted to marry her.

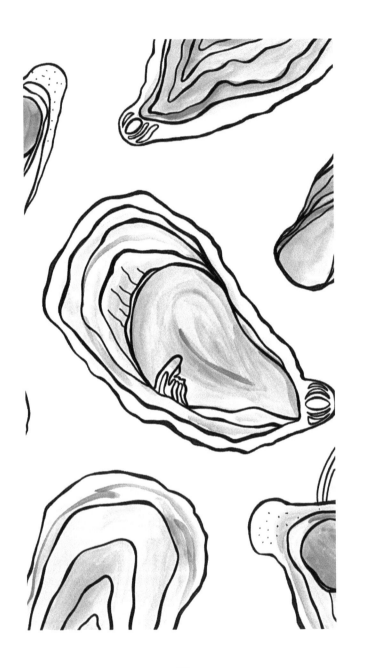

FIVE

(Megan)

Jonathan and I have joked about fate playing a part. I mean, I did love moving to California, but I always had a plan to live outside the USA, at least for a while.

Our first visit to Croatia was a vacation to mark Jonathan's 28th birthday. As each day passed, I fell for the place, for the culture, the lifestyle, the people. No, actually, not all the people. Some of the people.

As we were talking about fate, right out-of-the-blue, we met a Croatian guy who brought it all together and gave direction to what we were thinking.

We were always going to take another trip to Croatia. That was definitely going to happen because I knew early on that Jonathan loved being there. It was important to him so, of course, I was interested.

From the time we connected on Tinder, we connected well as a couple. We talked by text for a couple of weeks. Sometimes we swapped a couple of messages a day, then there would be more intense bursts where we were constantly in each other's thoughts. We really enjoyed exchanging ideas and seeing how some of them flourished into great conversations.

We agreed on lots of things, including how we felt our lives were a little stuck. But more than that, we agreed on the details of things. On blues and yellows and reds and dogs and wine and work and swimming and sailboats and the coast and travel and on having a good plan.

We agreed about things that looked awful, things that looked beautiful, things that looked like nothing at all and we agreed how they could be made to look better. We were often tying up the personal and professional and the passionate all in one stream and it felt good. It became inevitable that we would meet in person.

We were both dreamers, so what harm could it do to dream a step closer to each other?

In one particular message, I told Jonathan that I loved sushi. For our first date we went to *Sugarfish* in Santa Monica, which was perfect. Jonathan brought me a rose, which was a great little touch, and he had the chef's special and we ate it up. It wasn't until later that he told me he didn't like sushi at all. He ate a whole plate of sushi because he wanted me to feel comfortable doing the same.

We bumped into a couple of Jonathan's friends that night and had some more wine, lots of chat, and lots of fun. A couple of days later, we went to a concert at the pier in Santa Monica. We sat on the sand with a picnic, food and wine, among hundreds of others, and I remember it as such a beautiful evening.

My sister was there as well and we ran into her. The whole evening was lovely, fun, romantic. We toasted each other, danced a little, enjoyed the moment.

Our third date was in Orange County, where Jonathan was from. I went to stay with him for the weekend and it was perfect. No bullshit, no surfer dude games, no city slicker lies, just positive step after positive step.

I told him we had a pool growing up and that I had always liked the water and that was part of what brought me to California.

I mentioned that I had traveled to Europe but never as far east as Croatia.

My sister had been based in Madrid, Spain, while in college and I used to visit, stay for a while, and we would travel around. I was twenty-five at the time when I first visited her. I loved it so much that I promised myself I would travel somewhere different each summer. And that's what I did. I had a friend join me and we went wherever we could. Greece, Italy, France. We loved those trips.

When Jonathan said we should plan a getaway to Croatia some time, it was a no brainer. We were falling in love and I wanted to go to that place with the crazy brandy which had really spoken to him.

So off we went for twelve days in May 2015. And it was a continuation of the best things about our connection because he was right about it. Croatia was intriguing from the moment we arrived.

The main airport in Zagreb had almost nothing desirable. It was just like an old terminal building with some little customs booths. Everything was being written by hand and, looking back, it's funny how all that officialdom seemed quaint to us.

Everything seemed different, less hectic. I felt happy just switching off and really relaxing, opening up and seeing how far I would fall for Croatia too.

We found ourselves talking about how it was thrilling to people like us that a whole country still had all its own character in a world dominated by overlapping themes. We had fun making fake plans to decorate some of the stern old socialist era buildings and talking over the design ideas behind the adorable little houses and bars.

One thing I had to adjust to, which I hadn't been fully exposed to before, was Jonathan taking pictures all the time. And I mean all the time. Seriously, hundreds of pictures a day. He took the camera everywhere. Looked at everyone, everything. I'd be talking to him and then he was gone, shooting some lady in a market from a low angle.

Or he'd climb up high to shoot some old car from the 1950s or crossed the road to get a shot of me near some brickwork or a cat with a fish or a broken window frame that caught his eye.

Jonathan's a wonderful photographer. Compelled to keep catching moments, framing them in extraordinary ways. But jeez... he hauled an eighty to a hundred-pound bag loaded with lenses, and clutched his camera's handle grip so much of the time.

It had to be in his hands, he said, because he couldn't be one of those guys who had a camera around his neck. His dad always wore it like that and took terrible pictures anyway. Jonathan was trying to blend in better, put more effort in, take better pictures, and look like less of a tourist. I wished him good luck with that idea. He took around 5,000 pictures during that twelve day stay.

Do the math on that and you'd understand where I was coming from.

Yet we went through the pictures and they weren't just a record of where we were, but it's like he caught the sense and tone and attitude and temperature of everything in each shot. We had this kind of enhanced ability to look back at the path of our lives, and those enriching snapshots that really gave us a way to appreciate what we'd seen. It was cool, because no matter how awful things got, Jonathan's lens still found beauty.

We rented a car and drove from Zagreb to Dubrovnik, which was almost four hundred miles. We took boat trips with tourist groups out to the islands, and we felt like we didn't have the words to say how incredible it looked.

I talked about all those pictures, but Jonathan did put the camera away so we could soak it all in. And pretty much every memory I have of that trip was something close to perfect. It wasn't hot, more like fine and mild weather and it was off-season, before the tourists really started to arrive in numbers.

Things had changed since Jonathan's first visit out there. There'd been a lot of development in terms of the visitor market, but it still had so much of that old charm he had told me about. I told him I knew what he meant when he said it gets in the blood, right into the heart.

We didn't meet many westerners, mostly just locals, and we kept to ourselves anyway. We moved around in a kind of slow motion with Jonathan taking so many pictures, making the most of wherever we are. Sometimes we were the only people in the places we went to.

One of the things which stood out was the attitude we seemed to pick up from a lot of locals. It was like many of them weren't interested if we did try to reach out. Weren't interested in whatever business we might bring to them. We had people not acknowledge us, saw people look at us as if we weren't welcome, speak to us as if we had done something wrong. We had people literally turn their noses up at us. I'm not sure we'd ever encountered that straight-up rude-ness before. We were just rolling along in our happy bubble with no particular expectations so it didn't matter.

But we did figure out that not many people in Dalmatia were leaping out of bed in the morning all fired up to do a day's work, all super keen to help someone out.

Maybe there was an attitude in parts of Croatia that grew out of the social, political, and commercial divergence of east and west. Being Americans, we were treated coldly at times. Was it because of the way things have been over the generations? The way the stories of our different parts of the world had played out?

We didn't know. But when you're having the greatest trip and you're just crazy about the new relationship you're in, a shrug or a grumpy face or a micro snarl isn't going to get you down. A micro snarl can be kinda cute, in fact.

What I also remember was the random interesting and joyful people dotted around the place, people who contrasted with the surly and bureaucratic types. The fact was, every now and then, we would strike gold in terms of characters we met.

Our trip took us to the island of Hvar, a sort of Croatian Ibiza in the busy season, but it was the off season and we practically had the place to ourselves. There was this one older guy we met who was wearing a really stand out Hawaiian shirt and didn't speak a word of English. Jonathan has a really great photo of him. We got to speaking and he just kept saying *"Hawaii!"* every few moments and joking around, a kind of deliriously happy dude by default.

We also saw two guys talking in a little cabana, smoking cigarettes, and shooting the breeze. They were chuckling about Jonathan asking to get their picture, saying it was no problem. One of the guys was around our age and spoke perfect English. Michael had lived in Canada for most of his life and moved back to Croatia because of the changing times.

His family had taken him away as a little kid when war broke out, but he had always wanted to come back. He married the daughter of someone high up in the government in Zagreb and had insight into what was going on. It was interesting. A view right from the inside of a place which had caught our imagination. We ended up waving goodbye to the other six on the little boat trip and stayed on for a few hours more.

The conversations that followed changed everything. If we hadn't met Michael that night, the coming years of our lives might've played out differently.

He told us of a younger generation trying to make something of their land, who knew that there was little future in taking up the ways of the old men who rose each morning to sit all day. There's an attitude still around that came from a bygone time. A lot of people were working against that now, seeking to challenge the poverty of the generations before by opening their eyes to opportunities.

He said the young, just like the older people, loved their country. But the youth were talking more about ways to build new lives at home rather than how to leave their homeland behind like so many did in search of better jobs.

People knew that when the tourists came they didn't always see the best of Croatia. Tourists sometimes end up disappointed thanks to the ingrained attitude of the people with the grumpy faces.

But many were learning that when the tourists left, they should be going home as Jonathan had in 2006, with a desire to tell others about Croatia and with a feeling they'd been somewhere special and would be back soon.

Michael told us of an increasing focus on development both from the top-down and bottom-up across Croatia. He could feel the unstoppable energy coming to life. A whole country had finally got wings and the new Croatia, with its rocketing tourism figures, was a land with every reason to soar high and higher still.

We talked and drank and they smoked for three hours. We talked about the war, communism, upheaval, change, America, Europe, travel, airlines, hotels, the future and about why so many people smoked like crazy in Croatia.

By the time he took us back on his boat and dropped us at our hotel, an idea we had both been struggling to bring into words had formed.

By the end of that trip, Jonathan and I were talking about our whole lives together. It felt as if we had started designing a rock solid, yet romantic idea of who we were and what we wanted. We both knew Croatia would be the perfect location to achieve it all.

SIX

Croatia Journal: Zaton.
February 2016.

Our electrician was called Romeo, born and bred in Dalmatia. He had the loudest voice we'd ever heard. There's a story that his default volume had something to do with being struck by lightning three times. It suggested that his throat had been supercharged by the electrical bursts he kept attracting.

We weren't sure about any of that. However, we were sure that if you've ever been within a few miles of Zaton, you've probably heard Romeo.

He was in his fifties, a family man, and wore overalls with, it's said, nothing but Speedos underneath. There's another story that was going around that, when the weather's warmer and Romeo's working hard, the dungarees come off, leaving only the Speedos.

Which was just one more good reason to hope all the work was finished before guests arrived.

Yet despite all the shouty talk and that incoming risk of Romeo's ball sack in 3D, he was a great guy to have around. And that was a relief. We needed some kind of reliability around there. He was, as his name suggests, a romantic. He talked often of his wife, of fatherhood, of his three beautiful daughters, his wedding day, about how his family was so precious to him. We found it uplifting to have that booming voice bounce a Croatian/English blend of such sweet warm words around the hotel.

Our tiler was Branko, another middle-aged romantic, but his heart basically belonged to any passing female. Branko adored Golden Age Hollywood movies, loved to sing Sinatra and Presley and lost himself in thoughts of Bette Davis and Audrey Hepburn. He believed all ladies were queens and all men should treat them that way. He paused sometimes mid-conversation, fell suddenly silent, when he spied a pretty woman from the terrace or through a window or doorway. He put down whatever he was working with to raise a hand and cover his eyes.

"Oh moje oči," he'd say. *Oh my eyes.*

When the embarrassed female in question left the scene, he'd jump right back into the conversation as if nothing had happened. We figured he would get himself into a lawsuit pretty quickly if he lived in the USA, or at least a small part in *Keeping Up With The Kardashians*.

There was some good sense behind that buffer between work and play. We used to respect that line which said it's wise to keep the drinking out of office hours. Croatia taught us a great secret - it didn't have to be that way!

What problems could emerge when most of your workforce, power tools in hand, knock back rakija with the first coffee of the day and go on to drink beer for the hours ahead?

None at all...

A whole team of middle-aged men were at the hotel drinking daily. Those guys were balanced on platforms with drills, saws and hammers. There were constant concerns about wrenches slipping, blades slicing digits, dropped buckets of paint, and falls from scaffolding.

Not all of our workforce, just the ones who showed up. The others, the ones we made an agreement with and never saw again, were doing whatever outside of our presence. Fact was, we didn't know why they bothered looking for work there in the first place. Getting people to show up was actually a bigger problem than onsite drinking. It reached the point where we had booked two people to do the same job a couple of times because we knew we'd be lucky if one of them showed up.

One conversation was representative.

"Hey, so have you seen Ivan?" we said. "He said he would be here today to paint the window ledges."

A guy cracking a beer, taking a drink, gave a shrug and said, "No. Maybe Ivan is not coming."

"Oh shit. Why not?"

"He doesn't like working in the winter. Some people hate the outside when it's cold."

Confused, we said, "What?"

Apparently, some guys had a problem working in the winter because you could get your ass frozen off around there. That's totally understandable. We would just have liked it better if they brought that up when they agreed to work with us in the winter.

Anyway... right then just about enough guys showed up and, although the pace was slower than we would've liked, we were getting things done.

We learned quickly that we shouldn't give the impression we minded when someone rolled in with a six-pack or bottle of whatever in their backpack. We just said *'Cheers'* and hoped that their limbs stay attached to their body during the working hours ahead.

For the record, the work day was often about three hours, maybe four, sometimes five if you included the cigarette breaks. Fact was, all in all, we never truly knew who would arrive, at what time they'd arrive, how much they'd be drinking, what they'd do or at what time they'd leave.

Sometimes the place had been bursting with the happy sounds of hotel remodeling, of awful wood paneling being torn from walls, uneven floors being wrenched away, hammers hammering, drills drilling, tiles cutting. Branko would be singing his heart out (which he did all day) and Romeo would be casually talking in that booming, floor shaking way, until silence descended.

Then we realized our workforce had just vanished. Like messy magicians, they had left behind only a cloud of dust, beer cans, cigarette smoke, echoes of mom jokes (Croatians love a mom joke) and half-done jobs.

In those moments, we took the caps off, spit out the dust, made our way to the balcony, and breathed deep on that sewage-scented air which the government said it was fixing, and we wished they would hurry up.

Then we'd usually hold another of our short and increasingly intense management meetings. They went something like,

"Okay so... just remember it's beautiful here, right? That this is our wonderful new home, a statement about us, a launchpad for the rest of our lives. Focus on that."

"Yes. That's what we must focus on. And we must remember our hotel will take people's breath away, that we will make a great thing happen here."

"Yes. The problems right now are just the price we're paying to invest in our future."

"Correct. And we're maybe being a little too serious about this sewage smell. The local people are used to it so we'll get used to it too."

"Correct. And, quick fact, did you know that Croatia has had sewage since medieval times? Which means there's some history of expert plumbing, so I guess that smell over the whole bay will get fixed up when the plumbers arrive."

"Well, that's great. But you know the plumbers may never arrive, right? Have they been back since medieval times?"

"I'll look into that."

What we were trying not to do in our management meetings was yell across the bay, right into houses around the village.

"Forrrr fffffffuuuuuuuuucccckkkkk sssssaaakkkkeee! You've all gone home again?! Seriously?! Four hours on site, two of those drinking, and you've all gone goddamn shitting home?"

But, so far, we'd never done that. What we did instead was keep our counsel, stay calm, vent it all out a little as we breathed in a little more poo. Then we got back to doing whatever tasks our largely unskilled, totally sore, sometimes bloody hands could do.

We came up with a couple of strategies.

Strategy One was to retain the services of the people who show up and work for something close to a whole day. We made a list of those who did. Romeo was on the list. By himself. Sure, it was a short list but it was a work in progress.

Strategy Two was to stop being so damn polite and nice and behaving like we were still guests around here. This was our project and our money. We needed to get a little less nice. That too was a work in progress because, really, we were not looking to piss people off to the point we caused a walkout and got left doing it alone.

One of the most infuriating things in our world was that so few of these guys used email for their work. So few of them took calls or answered texts. We often couldn't call the ones who didn't show up. We usually couldn't discuss rates over email because that's just not how it was done. Getting used to that was maybe the biggest adjustment of all.

We just couldn't figure out why when a person has access to phone and email, they didn't use it to arrange any part of their working life. We couldn't understand why they wouldn't even activate their own voicemail when, as part of the career that paid for their home and fed their families, they were hoping to make some money. I guess that could be attributed to the old communist ways and how culturally different it seemed to us from the hustle of Los Angeles.

So, as you can tell, we were learning what we could about the working culture, about communicating with staff, about the humor, the jokes, the curses.

Here's one curse example. It's a great one. We think it's going to be pretty useful.

Jebiga!

Say it loud like you need everyone to hear.

JEBIGA!

It means *Fuck it!*

We'd really been giving *jebiga* some airtime over those last few weeks.

Within the first few days of getting there we met with Karlo, the owner, in Pula where he lived and where Niko and Andrea were from. That's in the Istria region, about four hours north and was known for its multitude of ancient Roman buildings, the most famous of which is the Pula Arena, one of the best preserved Roman amphitheaters in the world.

We gave him more detail on what we were planning, about the sort of people we would need to help us get there. He was super nice and said he would help in every way he could, but said we shouldn't do too much. He reminded us that, in his view, the hotel was in great shape as it was. We couldn't stress enough how wrong he was about that.

We told him we would be treating the building with absolute respect and that we were fully aware of its local significance. We said we would be starting with the bedrooms and asked him about his plans for all that junk he had stored in the wardrobes and up in the attic. It became pretty clear his plans did not involve moving it any time soon.

The three of us (including Sailor), planned to live in the hotel. That made sense because it kept costs down and we were overlapping with Niko and Andrea, our employees for the seasons ahead, who were moving out. We could get to know them a little better. We asked them to help with finding a few folks in or around Zaton and Šibenik who might be able to offer some skilled help – builders, painters, electricians, plumbers, tilers. Pretty soon word got around.

We were in the strong position of being able to promise people a lot of work so we asked for a few bids and got a few responses. But in the end, very little was agreed upon and, for whatever reason, no one seemed too enthusiastic. We got a couple of grumpy faces. Maybe it was something to do with the winter, maybe they just didn't like us and our crazy dog. Whatever.

So we started on the journey of showing this place some love ourselves. First off, we got stuck into stripping back what we could of those undernourished bedrooms. And the first part of that was to shift all Karlo's shit from the wardrobes. Almost as if someone was looking over our shoulder, Karlo found out right away. He sent word through Niko, his son, that he was seeking clarification about what we were up to in terms of relocating what could only be described as crap.

We resolved that issue and assured him we would store everything for now. Then we got word, once again via Niko, to say it wasn't just the old junk Karlo wanted us to keep for him, but also any new junk. The old floorboards, the ones that had rotted and splintered. The water damaged, weak and lumpy ones that had to be pulled from the ground. The ones that snapped as they came up. He wanted us to store all those too.

He wanted us to store up chunks of busted paneling and old window latches, and to never dump any old hinges or shelving brackets or wires or tiles in case he might need them for some purpose once again.

Basically, he was escalating an issue we had already tried to smooth out. A generous reading of his thinking would be that old Karlo was all packed with nostalgia for bygone times, and that he couldn't let go of even the broken and fragmented spikes of another era.

But, having listened to him speak a little off-guard about the way he handled his various business and property ventures, it was more a case that if he feels he can make half a buck from a pile of trash, he'll give it his best shot. It's that kind of mindset, we thought, that had been holding *La Perla* back. A lack of decisions taken, a lack of investment.

We told Karlo we were treating everything that was in good order with full respect, and that we too wanted to ditch as little as possible. But we were being realistic about the remodel, that decisions had to be taken, that if they were taken right, they never needed to be dealt with again. He didn't get back to us on that. So we moved it all to the old konoba, the disused bar/restaurant area off the lobby.

We intended to fix that up later. It seemed crazy to us to think that bar, with all the light flooding in and all the thirst in Zaton, hadn't been in use. And despite it having a large, unexplained hole in the wall (a running theme there) we could see so much potential in it.

Of course, all of what Karlo was doing was understandable. It was his hotel. Yet the issue was we'd talked on and off with him for months about our plans. We met with him three or four times, discussed it all, clarified the rental issues, showed him the renderings, and made our vision as clear as we could.

In turn, he made it clear he got it, that he knew the place had potential, and that it needed some passion put into it, to be reworked for the market now emerging online like never before. He got all that, signed us into a three year deal in which we would step forward and he would step back, where we would go to work and he would go away. And as the place was getting the makeover of a lifetime, we were really hoping he didn't keep looking over our shoulders and sending instructions from the sidelines.

But it was a complicated picture. It's not just a case that he was being unhelpful. It would not be fair to say that. For Karlo had been cool, had welcomed us to his home, had cut us some slack here and there, and linked us up with a few tradesmen.

Yet, a complicated picture kept emerging. A few times, he lined someone up for a job, and sent them to the hotel without even checking with us. We couldn't shake the feeling that the guys they sent had been prebriefed before arrival. That they'd been guided on what they should charge. We felt they'd been told about the rework plans from someone else's point of view before they even met us.

A couple of times we approached people randomly arriving on-site to ask who they were, what they did, how much they cost, how much they planned to drink in the hours ahead (it was good to have some insight).

It led us to laying in bed at night and, as that audible icy wind rushed right at us down the channel, we talked about how we were at the center of some kind of micro-economy here, that discussions were taking place about our finances beyond our knowledge. In our most paranoid moments, as the scent of the unfiltered excrement was blown around our room, we would say it all felt a little under-handed.

The good news, as we were telling people back home, was there were times when it worked out great with the tradesmen, and that was usually with the local guys. They started to pretty much show up on time. And they were open to the idea of giving us an accurate figure of how much they needed to be paid before they started, in-stead of keeping it as a surprise.

In other cases, workers wrote down what looked like an international telephone number, handed it to us, then advised that it was what they wanted for a week's work. We had a sort of laugh and handed the paper back, asked them to try again, told them we were not millionaires. But we were friendly about it all.

Right then, we were doing long days, working hard, taking breaks when we could, and keeping Sundays free whenever possible. We were seeing our plan take shape bit by bit, trying to keep cool and trying not to forget this was our whole new wonderful life we were chasing, not just some awkward project.

Sailor found some friends, but we weren't sure if they were a good influence on her or not. She'd been deliriously happy with her freedom there, thrilled she didn't have to be on a leash at all times like back home. People there were cool about dogs, didn't mind that Sailor was roaming around, and didn't get stressed about a perfectly pleasant mutt doing her thing.

She'd been good in that she stayed close most of the time, although on a couple of occasions we had to call out for her after she's vanished for a while. She'd come back and we wondered about some of those new pals she found, and hoped she wasn't getting herself involved with some troublesome canine street crew who'd talk her into rebelling against us. We wondered sometimes if she wanted to cause trouble because she was still pissed at us for drugging her, locking her in a box, and shipping her halfway around the world.

Niko and Andrea did move out, got themselves a little place in the village and had been coming and going ahead of the new season opening. For a few days the four of us were all there, all eating what we cooked on their two ring burner stove, just like we were camping.

They made some great local food for us, all sorts of things we hadn't had before. In turn, we made tacos for them, which likewise they had never had before. When they moved, they left the burner for us and with our limited time, total exhaustion, and otherwise bad cooking situation, we'd been having a lot of pasta.

To get a shot of happy sometimes we scooted over to Šibenik and grabbed pizza or a kebab and it tasted so good.

We liked Niko and Andrea, enjoyed their company in the evenings, and we missed all their nonstop smoking. Actually, we didn't miss the smoking bit and were looking forward to the day we could say smoking wasn't allowed in the hotel anymore.

And that other smell issue, that light aroma of shit from the bay? There was an official plan to resolve it for good, but apparently it was just a winter thing. It's some ecosystem issue that, we were told, would clear up in the spring. Fingers crossed.

Come Easter, it'd get a little warmer and we hoped everything will get a little brighter. *Porat*, the little restaurant next door, would reopen. It was co-owned by the man we saw being buried by the village the day we arrived. It looked really cool, that little place. It was just seconds from us, a little spot where we could grab hot home cooking and coffee. And man, we needed some good coffee. How could we be in southern Europe, in the neighborhood of Italy and Turkey, and not have good coffee?

Sailor was put to bed each night like a baby, even if she might be going through some teenage phase with her unknown new pals. She would get wrapped up in her blanket and she knew she was better off undercover, which was not normally a thing for a dog. But the loud, long, cold wind found its way right into our room at night and getting cozy was our only defense.

We were still waiting for the new shower unit to arrive so we could finally get some hot water. Taking a shower so far had been like shooting a scene for some horror movie about KGB torture, people all low-lit and frozen with terror, all blood-curdling yells and cries of *I can't take anymore* echoing around the building.

Karlo had said he would line up someone to fix the water heater but we said we'd just organize it ourselves. He agreed to pay for it. The problem was we were basically living in a building site and needed to wash these bits of walls and floors from our hair, skin, out of our ears and mouths and armpits and ass cracks.

Fact was it was tempting to not get out of bed some mornings, tempting to just hold onto the warmth of each other as the new, long, stupidly complicated day began and we were tempted to ask if all this was worth it.

You know... *jebiga... jebiga...* a couple of things had to change around there.

SEVEN

(Jonathan)

As far as learning Croatian was going, Megan and I were being coached mainly from the industrial strength perspective.

When people ask me to this day if I would speak a bit of the lingo I learned out there, I tell them what they can do with their mom and not much else.

Here's one I remember. It goes *Idiu tri pičke materine*. Romeo, Branko and the guys liked that one. It's basically, *You can go fuck your mom three times*, which is definitely a statement.

And there's one about your mom and a dog, some pigs, some other farmyard stuff. You get the idea.

I don't think there was a day in that crazy winter and into the spring when we didn't learn something. It was definitely cold, certainly colder than a guy from California is used to, and being inside the hotel itself wasn't much warmer than it was outside.

The snowfall had been pretty light, just a dusting of it around the bay really, like powder sprinkled over the little houses of the village and those high, landmined hills in the distance.

I was photographing a lot, stepping away from everything to frame up what was all around us, to focus on what's so easy to miss when your mind's elsewhere. I didn't ever want to lose curiosity about where we were. But we had pretty much zero headspace, very little time to sit back and appreciate what we wanted to appreciate.

We felt that there was a little tension between us and Karlo, as if some people working for us were actually working for him. There were some great days but then, other times, it just felt messy, as if we were doing something wrong when all we were doing, at great expense to ourselves, was doing what we felt was right.

Months had passed and I thought of it for a while as if we were being encouraged to give up. It felt like we were being invited to fail, to just walk away before the first guests even arrived. But that didn't make any sense. I had to put that down to being worn out, a long way from home, to being cold, and going broke, and being only able to communicate with locals about their moms.

I guess in hindsight, we should've been more aware, should have checked everything out, been less automatically trusting. Maybe we should've assumed some people wanted to take us for a ride. We were getting hit hard by the costs, getting pretty blunt approaches about work from people we didn't ask to approach us, getting the sense that other things were going on behind our backs.

I started finding it hard to get out of bed. I'd been disappointed, angry, frustrated, and worried all at the same time, many times. I'd been annoyed that sometimes it felt like no one gave a shit. A feeling that we'd been painted as some kind of enemy which would have been so insanely unfair. But that's how it landed on me, that's how it felt. I had some dark days.

There were times I didn't know what to tell people back home, what to say to Megan, what to think about it all. I would look out at that bay sometimes in the middle of some bad day and know I just needed to break away on that big cold water and to disappear for as many hours as I

It's always easy to lose track when the road ahead looks covered over. I guess I just needed to reboot around that time, to get up and running again with the same spirit that brought me out there in the first place. A big part of the issue weighing on me was that I had brought Megan to Croatia, that this thing we were doing came from something I introduced into her life in the first place.

And there we were, cold and a little confused and running out of cash too fast. There we were after having quit our hard-won careers to do something everyone told us was crazy. I tried not to let myself think they were right and I was wrong.

As that winter came to a close I knew I needed to get that hotel finished, that I needed a boat, that I needed a lawyer, and that, maybe most of all, I needed some weed.

(Megan)

WE were sleeping tightly together, Jonathan and I, all balled up, Sailor all wrapped up like a sandwich on her bed on the floor. When the light came I was able to feel it in Jonathan's body, just sensed that he wished he could stay for a while more, hang on to the warm honesty of rest instead of facing the heavy, deceitful day ahead.

I put the pressure on sometimes and was the one to cheerlead Team USA. To get my man out of bed and ready for work even though I knew exactly how he felt. We really did have this cold sense of isolation sometimes. It was like a gut feeling telling us that the more of ourselves we put into this the more we risked losing and that no one else gave a shit.

I was really looking forward to my dad coming out. He was going to stay a few weeks and would be helping with some of the vital work still to be done. He would be fresh support we could trust, another brain that would be thinking how to keep this whole train moving instead of not caring if it derails. He and Jonathan were to be working together on a few things, including building the bar. I knew it would be good for both of them, good for all of us. I couldn't wait to see him.

I had said to my dad by that time that it had been stressful, but that we remained committed. I told him we felt unsupported by a lot of people, as if we were being played, as if the whole thing could somehow fall apart at any moment. But I also said that we were building relationships, were not losing our heads or giving up, that we were going to take language lessons and get a good lawyer. I had said to him how I couldn't remember when the clamor in my brain about what and what not to do next was as loud and confused as it was right then.

He called me and we laughed about how as a little girl I would shun the Barbies and instead walk through each room moving cushions and tables and lamps around as he and mom and my little sister watched me do my thing. He said I had just gone ahead and became that same person as an adult, followed that instinct to assemble the environment around me and was never done until it was as good as it could be.

I had shown photographs to him, and to all our relatives, and told them all about the way we had approached this whole thing gently and openly and positively and respectfully. They were great. Jonathan's relatives, my relatives. We knew there was real pride back home in what we're doing, and that was important.

But it really lifted my heart when my dad looked at the pictures of what we had done so far and said we were doing it right. He said that just from the pictures it was like *The Admiral* was coming to life.'

WE had sourced an old Toyota for the equivalent of a hundred bucks and it made noises like no car should make, shook in places that no car should shake. We guessed it could fall apart or blow up at any second, but before it did it was useful for collecting people, getting pizza in Šibenik, for moving things from place to place, for sitting inside and tearing our hair out when we needed to.

It got us thinking about securing a hotel car, something with the logo along the side, something to catch the eye and that made some kind of statement about what *The Admiral* was soon to be all about. But the little Toyota would do just fine in the meantime. It'd put wheels under us, and pointing the car in any direction and making those wheels turn felt good.

We got serious about securing a boat, an essential part of what was to be *The Admiral's* offer. It would need to be a flat-bottomed craft to take future guests from island to island, out into the sea, a surefire way to get a little serenity.

Forming our plans around vehicles took us further along the road toward the goal because at least in that transport department no one could slow us down. Buying a car felt almost like a response to the negativity that had been knocking us off course.

Pretty much the first journey we took in the little old clunker was to the capital of Zagreb. At that time we could order almost no furniture online at all. We wanted to get to IKEA in Zagreb, and also to see if we could find somewhere a little more offbeat and original.

We drove for three hours in the hunt for faucets, light fittings, beds, tiles, and other stuff. Compared to L.A., the choices were limited, which was disappointing. But we were like excited children anyway, thrilled because the hotel we were staying at in Zagreb would have fresh food... and hot showers.

As the scenery changed, as the roads from Zaton to Zagreb became wider and the traffic got thicker, as our little wreck burped and rattled and we got honked at and tailgated and flipped off by the standard crazy drivers of Croatia, the skyline began stacking up.

For a while, we were comforted by the brief weekend return of a real, rising cityscape into our lives. We played tunes as we went, laughed about some of the shit we had been dealing with, talked about ordering room service. We wondered if we would miss having dust in our food, wondered how much peaceful sleeping we would do, about how hot the shower was going to be, about how many hours we would stand in it, about how many pieces of masonry and splinters of wood we would wash from ourselves.

Zagreb's a fantastic city, dated back to Roman times and had an easy, well executed blend of old and new. There were about a million people living there in really interesting little neighborhoods, along broad boulevards and tiny narrow streets, and it's got (almost) everything you could need.

We were definitely drawn to it, to the style of the young people (a lot less fanny packs and sweats going on), the sprawling markets, the upbeat attitude. It's got loads of museums, restaurants and, thankfully, better wifi than Zaton. Maybe it was because we missed the spoils of L.A. more than we thought. But we both knew we would make a point of getting back to Zagreb a little more, of getting some real urban pace into our lives from time to time.

In fact, we agreed on a few things on that weekend. These were things we needed to finalize now that we had torn down the paneling and torn up the worst of the flooring. The budget was shrinking fast and the bright fire of ambition in our bellies had threatened to dim. We agreed we would clear our minds, do some calculations, reconstruct the short timeline ahead, and discuss who should do what and who shouldn't do anything anymore.

We seared our skin in the shower and ate steak and drank wine and recommitted to everything, but this time with the benefit of at least some experience, this time with insight into what problems might lie ahead. We brainstormed a list of actions, listed the butts we needed to kick, told ourselves we should start by kicking our own. We talked of how we were the two people most invested, emotionally and financially, in this whole thing and had the most to lose.

We needed Karlo to get his act together and give us some feedback on what he was going to do about the kitchen. It wasn't fit for use, but he had made some early promises about upgrading the equipment. He needed to understand that the people he sent our way couldn't arrive like they were on some cash grab. That it was in all our interests for this crucial stage of the rebirth of the hotel to go smoothly and be done on time.

We also wanted him to get rid of the frankly insane collection of trash we were storing on his behalf. By then it was beginning to take over the bar area and we were seeking to turn that into an actual bar.

We decided to call him, visit, write, do whatever to get his full attention no matter what he might be thinking about us. We would secure ourselves some good legal representation and remind our landlord he had committed to letting us give this a go. We agreed we would say it to Niko, to Andrea, and say it every day until we got some positive movement on this.

It could be, that feeling all clean and relaxed and miles from the madhouse we had been living in, that we'd been too cautious about all this stuff. Maybe we had been too considerate, too polite, too much like nice tourists meeting people in their own land, as if we were always eating whatever was served, drinking whatever was poured.

We clinked our own big glasses of wine and agreed. Until this gets done, no more Mr Nice Guy.

We would warn the guys on the crew who weren't getting their work done needed to shape up.

We would decorate the place exactly to the extent and style of our choosing and anyone who didn't like it didn't matter.

We would put on newly mean faces when anyone handed us a cash invoice beyond what we had expected.

We would stop drinking shit coffee. Get some good stuff.

We would stage an intervention with Sailor, stop her from getting involved in any street gangs we didn't know about.

Within a few weeks the place was working better.

Example conversation:

Us: "That's like a month's pay for a week's work. You're joking, right?"

Painter: "Joking? Not joking."

Us: "Leonardo da Vinci wouldn't get paid this much."

Painter: "Leonardo da Vinci no good at walls. You want pictures of old ladies and Jesus? Get Leonardo. You want walls and window ledges? Get me."

Us: "We don't understand why you think we would pay this much? You want a serious negotiation? Give us a serious offer."

Painter: "But I was told..."

Us: "Who told you what?"

Painter: "Okay, okay, so how much will you pay me?"

What started as a figure four or five times what it should have been became something reasonable pretty fast via the medium of initial rejection.

We would often get the sense that the person had been advised elsewhere on how hard to go in, on how bold to get in terms of his demand. It became an illuminating process, adding circumstantial evidence to what we suspected that there was at least some amount of organization behind the attempts to hit our budget over and over again.

The painting took a while to get right. Everything needed to be done, inside and out, and progress was torturously slow. As newly resolved employers with a *jebiga* attitude, we had to take one guy aside after a few days. In his time with us he had gotten through maybe one can of paint and maybe fifteen cans of beer. We didn't set out to fire him but he got affronted at getting confronted. He exploded into a blur of arm waving, shouted something which, we're pretty sure, was about our moms. So that was the end of him.

Another guy complained his wages were short after a week's work. And that was a lie. We had the receipts. Sure, there were no contracts and initially there were no signed deals of any kind. But he had said he needed a deposit upfront and he got it. We had asked him to sign for it and it knocked him off course a little when he saw we had kept that receipt. We think he had assumed, or been told, we were rich and a soft touch.

Not today, friend.

So, word got around that playtime was over at the old *La Perla*. If playtime had continued, we would have been out of money and out of time as the guests started arriving.

But there was nothing we could do about the 'Being American' tax we had to pay that Croatians didn't. And that was okay. We were freshly resolute but still clued into the sensitivities of the situation.

By the time the remodel was coming to a close, we were staffed up with local guys, people we found we could work with best. There was something in those Zaton and Šibenik men that liked the idea of what was happening to the hotel. Some remembered the place from years back, remembered how their parents and grandparents danced and romanced and watched movies there. They knew there had been events of old Dalmatia and Yugoslavia within its walls which once stirred the soul and fired the heart. We got the sense that men like Romeo were proud to be helping turn the page for the new chapter of this old building.

As the spring embraced Croatia, as it greened the hills of Dalmatia and brightened the smiles of Zaton, as our little workforce became more engaged, we started to get the feeling something we hadn't seen before was moving into view.

Romeo in Speedos.

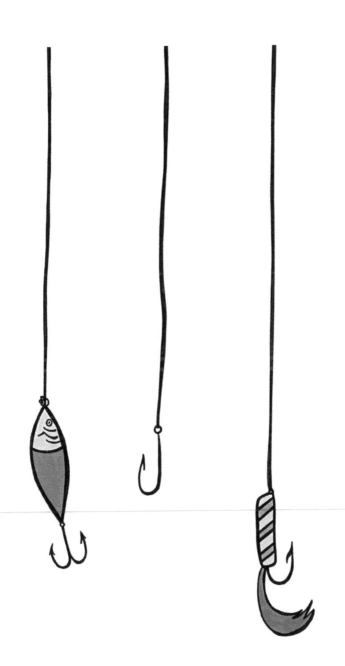

EIGHT

SOCCER'S the big sport in Croatia and the most popular game in the country. We didn't know much about the game but realized quickly it ran deep in the local community.

There have been leagues and clubs forever but, after the Second World War, Tito's regime created a bunch of new clubs and worked hard to whip up national pride via the sport. Today, by worldwide standards, Croatia is a big hitter. It has gifted the game some astonishing players - Luka Modrić, Alen Bokšić, Zvonimir Boban, Davor Šuker, and others.

The national team played in the final of the 2018 World Cup when we were there. France won 4-2 in the end. More than a billion people watched that game being played in Moscow – and that was one great day to be in Croatia.

There was a regular fixture, the *Hrvatski derbi*, when the two best clubs in the land, Hajduk Split and Dinamo Zagreb, hammered it out. It's a big deal across the nation and has been going on since the 1920s. Our loyalties lay with neither as we liked

Split and we liked Zagreb, and also because we were from a whole other place, but the rivalry got pretty fierce. There has been violence in the past.

In 2003, a guy called Zdravko Mamić took over as a director at Dinamo where his brother was the coach. He showed himself to be a real force of nature in terms of driving the team forward and upward in the years that followed. He became the single most powerful man in Croatian football and made riches from it.

Then, as is often the way of things, he was involved in some shady dealings. Sucked up a lot of the profits and authorised unusual contracts for players which gave him a cut of their earnings.

By 2014, Mamić was losing his grip on the club as the fans started turning on him. There were street marches in Zagreb with people calling him corrupt and demanding he get his ass kicked out.

A year later, he and some other guys were arrested on suspicion of tax evasion, bribery, and a whole bunch of irregularities. He was found guilty of taking around €16M for himself, which is about the same in US dollars. Maybe closer to $17M. And Mamić evaded a few million in tax. He was sentenced to six and a half years in jail.

The problem was that the guy figured it would be better if he cleared the hell out of there instead of going to court to hear the verdict. He packed up the night before and fled over the border to Bosnia and Herzegovina, where he held citizenship. In 2020, there was still no sign that the Croatians would be able to get him back and almost zero hope he'd ever go to jail. The Bosnians wouldn't extradite him because what he did wasn't technically a criminal offense in their country.

He was a wanted man, and a hated man in some parts. In 2017, he was shot in the leg in an assassination attempt. He was visiting his father's grave in Bosnia and Herzegovina at the time. Some masked guys ran out of the woods and opened fire, so it had been preplanned. Naturally enough, Mamić refused an offer to be treated for his injury in Split, back in Croatia.

No one underestimated how powerful Mamić remained, certainly no one in the Balkans region. He was friends with the president, with senior legal figures, judges, financiers, you name it. And, it's said, he was friends with some mafia style guys who didn't mess around when it came to getting things done. Some folks just didn't like the idea that people had turned against him, that the legal system had set out (and failed) to crush him.

We're telling you this for a couple of reasons. One was that the legal moves were being played out while we were in Zaton and affected the launching of our hotel. And also because, well, it's a heads up because our hidden away little boutique beauty would come to play a part in that crazy story.

Anyway, we weren't tuned in to any of that in the spring of 2016. All we were focused on was getting *The Admiral* opened in May. We had been sure that four months would be enough to get the people we needed, to get the remodeling done, to pitch our idea to the world, and begin attracting customers. But in April we knew it was going to be a close call.

Those four months seemed to go on forever, but as the days turned brighter and warmer, our hotel did too. As the potential of a new spring took hold, so did the promise of our — and we're not too shy to say it — awesome new creation.

We had drawn up a good sense of our offer on social media, a show-and-tell about what lay behind *The Admiral* and the part we wanted it to play in the lives of those who stopped by. We had placed more photography and video footage online, invited friends and followers to spend a while in and around the building. Time-lapse footage of the sun arcing over the south-facing bay beyond the hotel's three balconies said a great deal about the gift of our location. And pictures of us and the workforce rendered images of what the hotel was becoming and told a story of a plan coming together, of an end in sight.

The effort and frustration and concern that had been our daily bread had been giving way to a reemerging sense of excitement.

There was an interest and curiosity in our images and concept that sparked positive commentary. That led in turn to questions and feedback and interactions which we were only too happy to handle. We had been getting expressions of interest, fielding questions about the facilities, the building, the village, about Croatia itself, and it was as if it all validated the long, dark days.

It had become so important to us that people understood not just what we had been doing, but also why we had done it. We were thrilled to know people got it and could see what we had seen at the outset. The newest and, we were sure, one of the most amazing boutique hotels in the world, the product of our blood, sweat, tears, cash and a chunk of our sanity, was going to happen.

The photographs and footage proved it. *The Admiral* was coming.

We asked friends and family to help spread the word about our freshly-sparkling little gem with its fifteen spacious rooms and bay views. We reminded everyone who was following our progress about its cool combo of California chic and maritime aesthetic, about its light and bright and easy style, its turquoise, soft blues, whites, pale woods and wicker, of its casual class, how it was all about the professionals' playtime.

We enjoyed highlighting the rain head showers in each room, the geometric print rugs. We loved talking up the neat little closet areas, the nautical rope and copper bar curtain design which we felt gave everything an all-new sense of openness (given they replaced a host of busted wardrobes filled with old pipes, bricks, doorknobs, and tarpaulin). We loved showing what was planned for the *El Capitan* bar which was so close to being finished (given we had reclaimed it from disuse, turned it from a junk storage center to a very slick little hangout).

We said all this and reminded people they could come to this fine village and experience serious comfort in a reworked Communist Party meeting house of old Yugoslavia. We said how they could enjoy a slow drink and a deep sleep in a changed and changing place, how they would feel the rich sense of history as they read the untouched plaque on the wall outside:

Marshal Tito 08.IX.1953 visited Zaton to bestow this honor for participation in the people's revolution.

We emailed newspapers, magazines, and broadcasters to say we figured their audience might want to know about an extraordinary little boho beauty with a story. An ideal launchpad for hopping the islands just off the coast. There were dozens of sleepy, barely visited stop offs just beyond that gorgeous sun kissed bay.

Our little piece of happy was within easy reach of medieval Šibenik, and the magnificent tumbling waterfalls and natural forested wonders within Krka National Park were breathtaking. What, we asked everyone we communicated with about all of this, was there not to love?

As the remodeling moved from room to room and into the communal spaces of the building, we moved ourselves to the room with the hole in the ceiling. Its strangeness had begun to make sense. We had full use of the room and the little attic area above. Could get ourselves a little apartment with an upstairs bedroom, a warm and snug little private space.

The room itself, at the foot of the ladder, would become our office. It had been repainted, had new electrical outlets, and looked better than ever. Whatever madness we initially thought lay behind the idea of smashing a hole in the ceiling was madness no longer. We could physically separate our places of rest and work.

We went shopping for a spiral staircase, and splurged on ourselves. We made the hole bigger and slotted in those new steps. Only problem, which we had failed to consider, was Sailor. She had, we reminded ourselves, four legs. We tried, but she didn't take to the new minimalist design of the stairs at all. There wasn't much we could do about it. We accepted that, for every night as long as we lived in that place, we would be carrying our dog to bed.

All throughout the hotel, as new carpet and flooring went down, as new window frames went in, as new lights went live, it was like we could really see this place for the first time. We became less fearful of opening our eyes, less frustrated about the clear fact we would still not be fully done in time for opening because it didn't really matter. We had momentum and were within touching distance of realizing that enormous plan we had come up with less than a year before.

Jonathan was noticeably more positive but our feet had to stay on the ground. We had been cleaned out of cash and were running on almost empty. We had to be realistic about the season, how it could go really badly, that whatever happened we still had lots to learn about the business. We had the premises but we were still diving in at the deep end in terms of running every part of a working hotel.

Yet our spirits were high.

What was so great about the last stage of the remodel was the way everyone got fully on board. Our little hardworking team had gelled well, were all singing and drinking and insulting each other, and getting done what needed to be done. Romeo was effectively carrying them all along, keeping all eyes on the prize and making sure everyone knew they were doing a great thing in terms of bringing the hotel back to life.

As he joked around more and more, he began to draw the fire of the others. And to us, sometimes that fire didn't seem to be so friendly. We could hear him get ribbed by the others and could see that he was often the focus of the jokes. So, keen to keep tabs on any possible mutiny, fallout or other issues among the workforce, we asked Apologetic Andrea to advise us of any impending disasters we might need to know about.

"I can't explain what is being said," she said.

"Come again?" we asked.

She explained, "There has been a lot of joking about the little mark on the back of Romeo's head."

"Oh yeah, that little dent."

"Yes," she said, "Sorry."

"Wait," we said, worried that some past violent episode might be smoldering and about to bite us on the ass. "Is there an issue about the dent on his head?"

"No. Nothing to worry about I think. It's just that the others have been insulting him about it."

"Okay."

"They've been joking that the dent is because when Romeo's mother was pregnant, she was... what's the word?"

"Oh, yeah. Another mom joke. You mean they're saying...?"

"With the penis, very hard," she said, "they're saying she was done with the penis very hard when he was in the, what's the word...womb. And the mark is because... what are the words..."

"We get it. Thanks!"

"I'm sorry to have to be the one to tell you that. It's not true, just a joke."

"We get it."

MEGAN & JONATHAN RIFF

So we told Romeo we were sorry to hear the mark on his head was from a penis, but happy to hear that all was well with the team.

He laughed his big laugh and announced to everyone for about a mile around, "My mother said it wasn't true – but maybe I don't believe her!"

We had figured the dent on the back of his head might be something to do with him being struck by lightning three times. We knew that couldn't be true either. Like, who gets struck by lightning three times? So we told him that.

"It's true!" he roared. "Three times. Bang. Bang. Bang. Ouch. Ouch. Ouch. Yes. Hurts like hell."

"Oh," we said. "Holy shit. It's true?"

"Yeh," he said, shrugging. "It's fine. The penis on the head hurts more."

We had, by early May, gotten used to the Speedos. We're talking the skimpiest swimming gear on the most middle-aged of men. Romeo paced around with the confidence owned only by the sort of man who is totally happy with his life, who does not give a single shit about what you think of his post-prime ass cheeks or general sartorial choices. It was actually a little inspiring.

We could tell he was heartened by how it was all going and that he had no problem being used as some kind of lightning rod excuse, the pun for aggressive humor. He gave as good as he got. He told us he was looking forward to visiting the bar for a drink when the doors opened, and to spreading the word loudly about our hotel around Dalmatia whenever he could.

We had much to think about beyond marketing the place, beyond beginning to get excited about the upcoming opening of *The Admiral*. We already knew things could get a little bureaucratic in Croatia, and by a little, we meant a lot. It's said that all of it could be attributed to the legacy of the socialist era under Tito.

At that time, everything was theoretically owned by the state. Corruption was rife and everything was policed and documented down to the last paperclip in a bid to both counter corruption and facilitate corruption. The people in charge could do either and did both.

To work legally in Croatia, we had to get visas sorted out within sixty days of setting foot in the country. That process was one of the most frustrating things we had to deal with. Those still operating the legacy of those old bureaucratic codes had no regard whatsoever for just how bonkers it might drive service users. And the word 'service' was used there in its loosest possible sense.

The rules said that, with no room for changes, we had to employ four Croatian nationals and invest something like €30,000 {$36,000} annually into the country in order to run the hotel. No ifs, ands, or buts. So within those sixty days we needed help, and had to ask Karlo and Andrea and Romeo and others how we could go about getting people onto the books before we were even in business. We asked if we might be storing up problems ahead if every dot and comma wasn't in exactly the right place on the extensive forms we had to fill out.

All the advice had a similar theme. Get down to the visa office in Šibenik and give it a personal touch with whoever is dealing with us there. Give gifts, smile, lay on some praise, a little flirtation, whatever it took. This was the way to progress with all officialdom in Croatia, we were told.

We also were told that, in general terms, if we had any problems with the state, then the traditional way forward was to call on the most senior official, or even a judge if necessary, to make a decision. And before the decision was made, bribe the shit out of them.

"Did you just say that if we are having problems we should bribe the judge?" we asked our totally at ease with corruption advisor. "Yes, of course," we were told.

"In America, that's like one of the worst crimes you can commit."

"In Croatia, the only people who can't be bribed are the people you can't afford. It's the same in America. Don't lie. We know about the CIA and JFK."

"Okay, cool."

Sometimes we weren't sure where some people were getting their information from, but we would generally just let it go. Anyway, happily enough, we didn't need to look into stuffing a brown envelope with used notes and awkwardly sliding it across a table in the courthouse while hoping with every molecule in our bodies that the secret police, or even CIA, didn't barge in and we ended up being named across the web as the international criminals behind a criminal enterprise hotel.

So we visited a lady at the visa office in Šibenik and she was great. It definitely wasn't typical of us to arrive at a government building with flowers and chocolates and a willingness to do anything we were told, but that's what we did. It was pretty clear the woman we met was expecting a little treat. We had already chatted with her on the phone and she said we had to gather up all our information and passports, bank details etc. and go see her. But it was the mixed bunch of fresh spring flowers and the Swiss chocolates we brought, much more than the documents, that most delighted her.

It's just one of those little cultural quirks, one of those things that doesn't translate easily from place to place. Gifts were the way of things in Croatia. You went to someone's house; you brought a little gift. You met someone's wife for the first time; you brought a little gift. You needed help from your bank; you took a little gift. Need something official? Something unofficial? Go get some flowers, beer, whiskey, jewelry, mugs, cutlery, nick-nacks from foreign lands... It didn't matter so much what it was. The point was that's the way the meeting began, with smiles and a little positivity. It set the tone for what's ahead, and we found it very much more useful to play the game than step outside it.

The lady helped us and said we would have to put employees on the books as soon as we could and pay

even if we were not open for business. But, she said, placing the box of chocs under her desk along with, we assumed, dozens of others, there would be no checking up on her part. No official would be seeking interviews with the staff, there would not be any follow up pressure from her people. Basically she was saying she would smell the roses, eat the caramel, and tick the boxes and all would be well.

Some of our workmen laughed about it all. They knew that red tape was part of the problem for businesses in Croatia. They said it was one of the reasons so many people did things off the books.

Andrea and Niko joined in to remind us that sooner or later, as we already knew, the tourism department would be along to make sure the hotel was in good shape ahead of the new season. An inspection from some pen pusher was inevitable.

"It's the minister," Andrea whispered, "who will be coming." "The minister?"

"The government minister for tourism, yes. Sorry." "Gee," we said.

"Yes," she said. "You should know he is not a funny man and he will be drinking wine."

A few days later we picked up the same conversation with someone else, and talked about the minister coming to walk through the hotel.

"You know about the kitchen?" we were asked, nice and discreet. "Kitchen? We're not opening the kitchen yet. It's not fit for purpose."

"Exactly," our friend said. "Could be a problem." "Why? We're just gonna do snacks and stuff."

"I have heard the government might have handed over €60,000 for a new kitchen."

"What €60,000?"

"A grant to upgrade. Have you heard about it?"

"But," we said.

"You need to check if that is true."

None of that stuff about €60,000 sounded healthy. Was it true? If so, had it been paid? If so, who had it? Was any of this going to be a problem? Just as we were about to open our doors, were we about to find out we were players in some sort of government linked deal we knew nothing about?

A couple of days later a guy showed up in the lobby looking for the management.

He said, "I measure for the elevator." "Elevator?" we asked.

"Yes. Where do you want it to go?"

"We don't know anything about an elevator."

"Yes you do," he said. "Application for money for an elevator." "Shit," we said.

NINE

It was too late to be cautious about any part of this project. It was everything or nothing. It's not been just about opening our doors, it was about opening up the rest of our lives. We were going all in our way. Screw all the short-termism that was all around us, screw the lack of insight, screw the lies and half-truths, just screw everyone else. We were going to make this work for us.

We'd chosen a quality PR company in London to help get the word out, to drive our message towards the right publications on and offline. We needed help to tailor what we needed to say because no one else was going to help us reach out to the market. We always knew that we needed to target an adventurous younger, aspirational crowd looking for something special, looking for, not just a room off the beaten track, but a story too.

The plan was to open in mid-May. A couple of extra weeks would have been ideal in terms of finishing up, but a couple of bookings had been made and we'd been excited about honoring that. But we could hold on forever trying to get everything perfect.

An interview was lined up with a website called Šibenik News and went live. A photographer came along, got some shots of us in the lobby and bar. It was a little too early at that point to really show off what we had done. The images came across a little bit building site chic. The website's English version also seemed a little like a work in progress, but we thought it made the right impression.

It reported: *The Admiral Zaton, whose name came from Jonathan, stands on the site of what was once La Perla, which has been completely redesigned from exterior to interior whose design is by Megan, who is, in fact, a professional.*

It told how our falling for each other was followed up by falling for Croatia, and that this American couple had *packed their suitcase and arrived at Our Beautiful.*

It talked of the place having a *Mediterranean touch, for which the most deserving motive must be imbibed through shades of blue, anchor motifs, while using materials of marble, metal, and wood.*

The redesign of the hotel helps locals, among whom they have found a workforce, and the atmosphere in the hotel is comfortable, despite the fact that the works are coming to an end as the tourist season and the language barrier nearer, i.e. they combine Croatian and English on both sides.

As they speak, neither of them has mastered the language, but they both understand more than they can speak, with Jonathan giving Megan an advantage in knowing the new language. Megan is honest, whose winter in Dalmatia is not particularly popular. Neither Megan nor Jonathan are surprised that the hotel rooms will not gap.

We could not have put it better ourselves.

We went public on May 16 to say that our hotel was open for business. We figured we were sixty percent ready to roll. One obvious issue was with the televisions in the rooms, in that we didn't have any. We bought in bulk, and wanted one for each room. We had space marked on the walls and everything was ready for connection, but there was nothing to watch.

Ahead of our first guest arriving, we shot off to the store and got one for their room. And a mini fridge too. Because none of those had arrived either. Likewise, space was marked out but there was nothing to fill it because of more delays from our suppliers.

But we were pretty sure our first guests wouldn't be too tough on us if everything wasn't perfect. They were friends with Megan's parents. A Californian couple who'd been looking for something new to see and do on vacation. Their arrival was testimony to the most persuasive advertising of all – word of mouth.

We were up at the break of dawn on arrival day, cleaning and polishing, perfecting our super chilled out front of house faces despite the million things going on in the back of our minds. Niko, Andrea, and we wore matching staff outfits we had picked up at H&M and Zara in Zagreb to work as uniforms, to give us a nautical summer look. The women were in black and white barcode striped pants, white T-shirts. The guys were in blue shorts, blue and white striped tees, short-sleeved light denim overshirts. Sailor had a bath and wore a new blue collar.

We checked and double-checked their room and left a nice bottle of wine and snacks out and spent a couple of hours feeling super excited ahead of their eleven-a.m. arrival time. We were going to be able to say 'Welcome to The Admiral' for the first time.

We cleaned up and reworked the kitchen so it could serve as a base for serving snacks ahead of developing the restaurant. Some secondhand equipment had started to arrive thanks to Karlo, but it was still far from being somewhere a good chef could work. We figured his sudden interest might have something to do with the story we had been told about the €60,000 {$70,000}.

Whatever was going on there was our landlord's problem, not ours. We hadn't planned to open as a restaurant in 2016 anyway. A restaurant would just be another thing to worry about, another part of this whole thing to staff up and manage at a time when we were seeking to take baby steps. Our bar was open for drinks and coffee, so it wasn't like we had nothing to say in terms of refreshments. And the cool little café *Porat* had opened up next door so we could direct hungry guests there in the meantime.

The guy who came to see where we wanted the elevator was handled by Andrea after our initial confusion. She seemed to think Karlo would have some knowledge of what was going on with all that. We didn't need or want an elevator, but it turned out there was an application for one which just maybe might've secured the support of some government funding. But we didn't know for sure, and never found out.

Andrea talked to Karlo and came away saying it was just an idea that was being looked into now as part of future planning for the hotel. Maybe we could take that at face value and just consider it to be a vote of confidence in what we were doing with *The Admiral*.

So eleven came and went and there was no sign of our first ever guests. The four of us got some lunch together, considered how it was still a little cold on the terrace, talked about how great it would be when we got the boat, and didn't talk about kitchens or elevators.

We considered putting a call in to our expected guests, just to check if everything was okay, to check if they were lost or needed help, but we stepped back from doing that after a while. Maybe it was too early to give them the idea we needed them to show up. There could be any number of reasons why they hadn't arrived.

In those first hours, across those first couple of days after opening, we became a little bit of a draw from passing locals. From curious people around the village. And we were reminded in that period that Croatians could truly be straight talkers.

One guy walked into the lobby, looked around, walked up to us and said he didn't like the shutters. One woman came in, looked around, looked at us, walked right back out as if she had been insulted. One couple entered the bar, said they were glad to see the old place back up and running again, and wanted to see if we would be open for morning shots of rakija around seven a.m.

"Sure," we said, not knowing if that was legal or even moral, but at that stage we were keen to secure a customer.

Around midafternoon, still with no sign of the guests, we let Niko and Andrea go for the day. They had genuinely been as excited as us to welcome the inaugural tourists, but it made no sense for us all to be there with no one around. When it got too late in the afternoon, we went ahead and put a call in. There was no answer.

We asked each other, "As hotel managers should we really be calling up guests who haven't shown?"

An old lady walked in during that debate and explained in broken English that her wedding reception was right there and that she got married in the little *Church of St Roko* in the square outside. She was emotional about the place getting this overhaul and it was comforting to hear her story. She wiped away a couple of tears and said she would come by some time with her wedding album and we could see how it was back in the day.

We told her it would be an honor to see it. And then she asked if we had any trouble from the youths who hung around in the square in front of the church in the evenings, just a little further along than us. We said there had been no issues.

"I hope they do not bother your guests," the lady said.

We had noticed before how a little knot of teens met up there, but we had never had a problem with noise, never been hassled by them. We had noticed too that there was a cafe bar just across the way and figured it might open up soon and might be a draw for the younger people. The lady said we might notice a few changes now that the season was getting underway. She said that the young have very little respect for the older people.

We actually didn't feel that way at all and actually felt that the teens we had met had been good-natured. It had been tempting to say, "No we haven't noticed the teenagers hanging around but, damn, have you seen all the old guys who sit around outside on boxes shooting their grumpy shit all day right across Dalmatia?"

(Megan)

"It hit us around ten p.m., at the end of a long and pretty disappointing day. I could tell Jonathan was tired and I was whacked out too. The expectation had been fun but it had turned to nothing. Our first guests had not arrived.

I guess it was a day to remember really for the wrong reasons. Truth was, we couldn't work out what had happened. We had checked our guestbook, the date, the arrival time, left a message, and had no response.

Sure, they could have kicked back in Zagreb after arriving. They could have had a few drinks, taken another room somewhere for the night. That was their choice.

It was kind of funny that instead of our guests arriving, some random people were coming and going through our doors all day, putting their heads into the bar, asking if we would have music nights, if we would be making some good cocktails, asking how much they would cost.

All that time, we had been focused specifically on getting our guests inside, showing them their great room, treating them right, and getting some real early feedback.

I figured I could get in touch with mom and dad and ask if they knew anything about their friends' plans, but we didn't want to worry them.

Anyway, it was late and it looked pretty clear no one was coming.

I said to Jonathan that, if he didn't mind, I would go up to bed and suggested he do the same. But I had a feeling he wanted to sit it out just in case.

So he said he would wait for a while and catch up with me later. I left Sailor there with him for company. I knew I just wanted to close my eyes and think about tomorrow holding the answer to what had happened, about looking forward to a better day.

(Jonathan)

MEGAN went to bed and I took Sailor on a walk around the hotel, over by the bay. Let her do her night-time business and get some air.

I was unsure if I should get a beer or just lock up the hotel, if I should just go join Megan upstairs, or wait around for a while.

How long should we stay open for guests who were twelve hours late anyway?

Some of the teenagers were at the end of the alley in the little square, goofing around with each other, laying on some benches, drinking a little, smoking. Looking around, I could see they were within earshot of maybe half the rooms of the hotel and I'd been thinking that it could become a problem. But I guessed there was nothing much else for them to do and no other place for them to go. I walked by them with Sailor, nodded, and they said hi.

It was getting towards eleven thirty and I was going back inside and this guy I had met before, Tomislav, called out. He had been walking through the square and saw me and the dog. He worked at the harbor and had dropped in to see what was happening a couple of weeks back. He knew Romeo and some of the other guys we knew too. So I looked over and he waved his hand, and took something out of his standard Dalmatian fashion accessory, the fanny pack.

"Hey Jonathan," he said.

"Hi Tomislav."

The handshake, something passed to me.

I said, "Oh," and I was confused.

He said, "It's yours," and nodded, then said, "I heard you needed to relax."

I looked and it was a little baggie, filled with a little weed and some papers.

"Oh, man, right, great. Thank you. Can I..."

"No," he said, "this forget. This help for the way, if yes for you. No problem, no problem. Welcome Dalmatia. Hotel is and for okay?"

"Yeah man, all good with the hotel, really good."

"Season is, eh, now. Season now? Everything busy now. Open?" "Yes, open. Still a lot to do but guests are coming and we're pretty sure they'll enjoy it."

"Great, great. No problem. Do the call me, okay? I know best people. I send over my friend Josip and he can help when you get boat."

"Oh great," I said. "Yeah, I need to talk to someone about that."

"No problem, no problem."

So that was unexpected, but I can't say I didn't welcome the idea of a little weed. At the same time, it proved that everyone talked to everyone, that Zaton was a hard place to keep a secret. I mean, I had spoken to one of the guys doing some work about how a lot of people smoked weed in California, and then this other guy approached me from nowhere. I guess, in that case, it was all good!

I had to say that I took a little rest on the terrace right away, sat down, and chilled out, soaking up the surroundings. I had a little crazy smile break out on my face by the time I went back into the lobby. I figured I would give it until midnight and then go to bed.

I got to thinking back to my degree in Tourism Development and Management and about interning at the *Montage* hotel group in L.A. And wow, how amazing that was! They had twelve resorts, all five stars, all five diamonds, all just incredibly beautiful, inspirationally beautiful. I had interned for about six months with *Montage Laguna Beach* and was involved in every department, and I had really taken a lot from that experience. Most of what I did with those guys was marketing, and what I learned had been with me all that time.

Maybe that was part of why it felt vital to me that *The Admiral* was not just a place to stay but that it had a tone, a mood, a reason to be wanted, an extra quality about its quality. It was important that it had something that bled contagiously, smoothly into the mind and that every mind could in some way connect to what it was about, that every individual could have some measure of individual experience that flowed from Megan's ideas, my ideas.

I knew there was a way to have beautiful physical things bond fast and clean, to create a link to the senses right from the walls and floors, from the décor, from the location. I guess every hotel would want the same and would say something like that in their marketing, but for me this mission we were on had become personal. It was as if everything in my past was meant to take me to that point.

I was taking inventory right then and there in my heart and was honestly amazed at this thing we had done. I was thinking, no matter how crazy it sounded, that silent time was like a punctuation mark in my Croatia experience, like the moment when I realized I was at the ending of one thing and at the beginning of another.

It came to me that everything I loved was with me now, partly by design, partly by chance. It was totally clear to me that Megan and I really had been fully, jointly aware of the potential and that we had taken something that had been fading away and made it glow.

I was sure that if I walked past this place with my camera that I would come in, like all those other curious people had been doing, and I would need to get pictures. I guess you could say I was a little emotional, that everything that had been moving around and making noise in my brain was now still. There was a moment of huge happiness and satisfaction inside the silence.

Upstairs lay the greatest girl I had ever known, the greatest beauty of this whole thing, the most astonishing creator, the strongest fighter, the most dependable partner. She had become part of it all, understood it all, wanted it all too, made it all come into existence, never accepted that it would not get done. Without Megan this wouldn't have happened at all.

I knew I was so in love with her, that I wanted to spend all my spare time with her, all my working time with her, all my hours and minutes and life with her. In my bird's eye view of my world that night, after months of just trying to make it from one day to the next, I could see clearly how she was at the center of everything that had taken place.

I was curled up on a soft chair and fast asleep when the guests finally arrived. I woke up, just after midnight, and they were standing there, all smiles and luggage, all cheery and ready to checkin. I woke right up and the first thing I said was, "Holy shit."

They said, "Hi."

He reached out to shake my hand as I got up. I apologized and said that we had been expecting them earlier, that I didn't expect to fall asleep, but it had been a long day.

They looked around and said the place seemed great, that the village looked stunning. I said that in the morning they would get to see how gorgeous it really was there, that we felt lucky to wake up there every morning. They seemed delighted, and that they were looking forward to their break. It had been a long flight and they wanted to just go to bed.

I signed them in and asked what they had done all day. They said not much other than sit on an airplane. Turned out they weren't late at all. We had got our times wrong. We put their arrival time down as a.m., but it should have been p.m. Not the kind of mistake we needed to make again. A lesson learned.

The guy said how they were friends with Megan's parents, but didn't know her themselves. I told them she was great and saw them to their room. I was happy to see them pause after they went in, to see them look at the new bed and new flooring, at the whole new frame around what would be the most beautiful view when they woke.

I went back down, locked up, called Sailor, and headed for our little space at the top of the old meeting house. I couldn't wait to tell Megan that our guests had arrived and that our adventure was continuing. That we had somehow got the timing wrong. I couldn't wait to say that I had been able to step back for a moment and take everything in and that I was so excited about the whole season ahead. I wanted most of all to tell her I loved her.

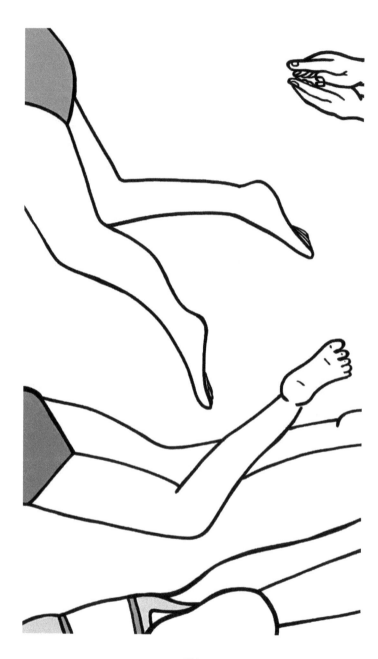

TEN

Croatia Journal: Zaton. June 2016.
(Megan)

JONATHAN was a little less surefooted on our spiral staircase that night when our first guests arrived. But he was happy they had shown up and was buzzing with everything that lay ahead, delighted with his new friend Tomislav.

It was great to see him so positive because I had a few negative things on my mind. Our relationship with Karlo had been really starting to burn, just in the sense that it didn't feel transparent at all. We had stepped beyond his shadow to some extent and just got on with what we needed to do, but if we didn't get every detail cleared up could it mean problems ahead?

We knew the market better now and that the rental agreement we signed at the outset was over the top. We should've fought harder for a better deal. We did get commitments that the landlord would pay for certain parts of the remodel. That we would agree on details and fix it all through the leasing arrangement, but there'd been a real pull away from that now.

Karlo frustrated us by saying we had been doing too much. Yet he had seen the renderings, talked in person with us, and could be in no doubt about our ambition.

I figured that if, for whatever reason, he truly never did understand that to turn *La Perla* into *The Admiral* took major change, investment, and a little bit of faith all round, then I could only think he didn't understand tourism. If he didn't get that it was not just about providing a bed, about the human value of the experience and the exponential power of the overall message tourists took away with them, then I figured he could never learn.

But on the upside, we had a lawyer looking at the contract, and into everything. We had also opened the doors and just welcomed our first guests. And, maybe greatest of all, the entire hotel had working showers! We also contracted out a high end espresso machine with some real coffee, which provided better fuel for the new morning routines. We had that thing bubbling at first light and the scent filled the air as a kind of smoke stink replacement. As a way of covering the wafts of sewage, although, as had been promised, by springtime those wafts were fading away to nothing.

But what about our new morning routines? What do you do in the morning when you run a hotel? It seemed obvious, but when you had a long list of little things to do it was easy to overlook one or two of them. Niko and Andrea had been a great help with that. They willingly did whatever they could, anticipating our weak points and showing us how it was done.

Jonathan and I had managed projects before, up to and including the remodel, but neither of us had ever managed a whole hotel. I took on the back end of things, and got us on *Booking.com* and and learned what I could about bumping up our presence, about making the best offers, teaching myself how to run seasonal rate discounts. It was complicated.

We were a few weeks in by that time, taking on new staff, heading towards full capacity and it was getting scary. I got the feeling there would be errors ahead on my part, on Jonathan's part. We worried a little because we really didn't want anything to ruin anyone's vacation I booked a couple of webinars on the online management process and was really hoping it all started to make more sense.

Basically, I had no freaking clue how to run a hotel. We had people calling in and emailing and booking online and needing details about things we'd never heard of. We were getting questions about leaving and arriving in the middle of the night, demands to change lightbulbs and make the beer colder and about discounts and for information about Tito and the islands and history of Šibenik and how to say whatever in Croatian and if we could pick up their bicycles in Split and change their money and rebook them because they wouldn't be coming next week after all.

I mean, I could handle guest relations like a pro, but pretty much all the behind the scenes prep and insight and organizing was going to be learned on the job.

We realized a couple of weeks before that we would really need some quality transport. That our little Toyota was never going to be enough to keep up with all the errands we needed to run. We'd been lucky to pick up an old, very old, Land Rover Defender which, with a little work and a lot of luck, might get us through the season. I had to say it looked so good with *The Admiral* logo along the side, and the expense had been worth it. We lined up ten guest bicycles too, and hoped to get those branded as well.

Before we opened, we had to get certified by the city of Šibenik so we could be officially listed under the new name. There was a lady in the office we had to see about getting the hotel checked out to make sure it met their standards. What we needed to be sure of was that we would get marked in as a three-star property. Obviously that's not the highest but it's the highest we could go because we didn't have a pool.

We wanted all this to be a fast and easy process because it was vital for our business. We had heard stories about it sometimes being a process that did not go smoothly and we didn't need that in our lives. We figured it was possible, for whatever reason, that if someone in the system was against us they could delay or downgrade us and leave us high and dry. We knew the office was busy too and that people had ended up sitting for hours waiting for appointments to take place.

I said to Jonathan, "This needs to go right. I'm thinking of roses and chocolates right from the start. We need to win this lady fast and full."

He said, "That's true. And that's why I'm thinking of going in even harder. I'm thinking of... perfume."

And that was some good thinking. An attack on three fronts: flowers, chocolates, perfume. Really, the plan was to break down any resistance, Croatian style. She would be putty in our hands. And, yes, I was happy to say that's how it worked out.

We talked super nicely to her on the phone and she saw us pretty much right away, which was great. We showed her pictures, talked enthusiastically about our dream, and raved about us giving a little boost to tourism in the area. We talked to her about how dreamy the perfume was we had just invited her to wear. She laughed at that.

She made an appointment to see *The Admiral*, walked in the door smelling great, beamed her big smile again, and said it all looked fine, signed a document, and handed it over. I'm happy to say we got our three stars.

Next up was the Minister for Tourism, and we figured that wasn't going to be as easy given those stories about him being as charming as a wasp. We had asked for him to come back during the remodel but we had not been given a date. His job, we were told, was to come along with a checklist, to walk around and tick boxes, to satisfy himself as to the hotel's fitness for purpose in line with all the various regulations.

We got word from his department a few days ahead of him showing up which gave us time to get ready. It was at that time that some more (second hand) kitchen equipment began showing up, getting put in and polished up pretty fast.

On arrival day we uncorked some of the best wine we could get and made some very fine charcuterie board and snacks, and considered (only half-jokingly) placing a bottle of cologne or a bunch of cash into his hand.

One of the numerous little issues on our minds were the king-size beds we had sourced in Zagreb for many of the rooms. Turns out, king size wasn't a standard size in Croatia. It was only after we took delivery of them that we realized we couldn't easily source sheets to fit.

We asked a small company from Zagreb to make some luxe cotton sheets for us, which they did. But, for reasons we couldn't totally work out, the sheets were too short. We had to send them all back explaining we were confused about what their king size was compared to our king size. We were surprised when the same sheets came right back to us with an extra bit sewn onto the end. We wondered if the notoriously picky Minister for Tourism would be looking at the bedsheets, if there was a possible issue there. We really had no idea.

The minister arrived with one very serious face, as we had expected, and one assistant. He was checking against the list of things he had already seen the last time he was there a year before, ahead of the management changing hands. We truly didn't know what he would be looking at in particular because the feedback from Karlo wasn't clear. So we just let him do his thing. He looked unimpressed by everything, said very little, got himself a glass of wine, and took a wander.

His word really could make a difference, positive or negative, and we had no recourse if he hit us with some unwelcome news.

A lot had changed since his last visit, and the hotel was certainly cleaner, lighter, less damp, less smelly, and now no smoking was permitted. The new water heater was in, which may or may not have been an issue for him. And the kitchen had improved but wasn't exactly what you would call state of the art.

We didn't know how that might affect us if he got to examining the (second hand) oven, grill, and other units, but we figured our landlords would handle that.

So he walked into the kitchen, looked around, and just walked out. Jonathan and I looked at each other not knowing what that might mean. He walked around the lobby, the bar, strutted about upstairs, checked out all the bedrooms. At the end, he turned to us both in the hallway, his face upset, even a little angry, and called us to one of the rooms.

That nautical rope and copper bar idea, basically our cool closets, had been our way of separating wardrobe from bedroom. He pointed at one, said, "This is not Los Angeles. If you are traveling with your partner, nobody wants to see each other's undergarments!"

We said "Well, of course."

We said that we hadn't thought it through, and that he was so right. Then we offered him another glass of wine. He said we would have to change it all up, bring in a load of proper wardrobes, and that we should get that done pretty damn fast. We didn't think there was any reason for him to hold off on our rating.

We asked if he would like some pancetta or more wine.

He didn't take us up on that. I smiled as he handed me his glass and I told him we would really look forward to seeing him again.

Jonathan said a few minutes later after he was gone, "About that 'change all the closets right away' instruction."

"Yeah," I said, "that's not gonna happen."

But it had been those less than official visitors who had been the most engaged with what we'd done there, with who we were. A few days before, two older men showed up looking a little furtive. They approached Jonathan and asked how long he was planning to stay in the area.

Jonathan explained we had no answer to that. He said depending on how things worked out, *The Admiral* might be the first of a number of *Admirals*, but that this was all an idea in progress.

They asked, "Not going back to America?"

Jonathan said, "Yeah, sure. We'll go back to see everyone at the end of this season. Why do you ask?"

One of the men said something like, "People think you might be running away from America."

When Jonathan questioned that, the guy said, "I think no one would find you here for a while if they were looking."

We had to ask each other what the hell that was about. But it was part of a pattern of suspicion, a running theme where people were wary of our motives, our background, wondering why we would come from California to Zaton without some negative force pushing us this way.

There had been a real sense at times that people figured we were shady, that no matter what we said there was an assumption we'd been up to no good. Some people in the bar jovially asked if we had any military or intelligence contacts in the area since the American involvement during the independence war. We figured there wasn't much we could do about any of it, that we'd just let people think what they wanted to think, that it didn't make much difference anyway.

We laughed a few times about how some might consider us some kind of gangsters, runaways, a *Bonnie and Clyde* couple. They might have been wondering why we would relocate to eastern Europe while the relocation template to date had very often been people in eastern Europe relocating to the USA. We could see how the rumor mill might turn in our case.

The queries had not just been about us, but also about our landlord. Karlo owned quite a bit of property which he had plans to develop. He had at least one working hotel on his books beyond *The Admiral*. But it had been the emergence of our hotel, and more specifically its standard, that seemed to get people wondering.

We'd been asked how close we were to Karlo and if he was still the owner. And about some of the business partners he'd had over the years. We were asked details about our role in the remodeled hotel, how we all got around to meeting each other in the first place. We got the impression that some people had a lot to say about Karlo, and others weren't quite sure if they could trust us with what they wanted to say.

We decided it would be in our best interests, and would also be enlightening, to ensure we were considered as independent as possible. We needed to be seen as our own people running our own business, and that Karlo was not part of the picture in our personal lives.

So it actually looked like our really cool little *El Capitan* bar could become something of a draw for locals, a place to drop in and discuss the latest rumors. And obviously we could reasonably expect our guests and other tourists to drop in too. That nightlife side of things had led us to lock in ideas about regularly hosting bands and putting together what we wanted to be the best cocktail list in the area. If people were to find that our bar catched their eyes, a little speakeasy in a building that still meant so much to many in the village, then we would make sure they felt welcome.

We sounded out some local folks we had been getting to know, getting to trust. We wanted to hear about local musicians, about local drinks. We were getting other recommendations all the time. The Olympics were on, the sun was shining and it was going to be great.

In terms of the bar, a key issue had been figuring out the right price point for the drinks. A new friend called Josip, was a fisher man and olive grove worker who was introduced to Jonathan by a mutual pal. He was well informed about that stuff. He had a fanny pack, wore sweats, and had a stern face thing going on, so we knew for sure he was Dalmatian and knew the ground.

His answer to our question was pretty much, "You must the people tourist price also before local the price."

I guess it's fair to say his English sounded like a string of random words yet still made sense.

"Okay," we agreed, "so you mean one price for locals, one for tourists?"

"Kindly," he said, nodding, "but outside write no."

"Okay. What?"

He did a thing with his hand, indicating writing, then shook his head.

So I said, "Oh, I see. We can't write about the different prices on the board?"

"That," he said, nodding.

"So how much cheaper is the drink for a local than for a tourist?" He shook his head and said in a sort of educated tone, "Very times the people!"

We looked at each other, unsure.

I said, "You mean it depends on the person?"

"That," he said, shrugging. "Prices, people, sizes, times, days, jobs, depends."

"Shit," I said. "This could get confusing."

"Correct, no problem," he said.

"Hey," I said, thinking I had hit on a good idea. "Would you like a job in our bar?"

"No," he said.

ELEVEN

(Jonathan)

THERE was no smell of sewage over the whole season. Megan and I had gotten used to it by the end of the winter, but in the spring and summer it faded away to nothing. It wouldn't be back until the end of the year when the tourists had left.

The weather was perfect in that summer of 2016, and had been becoming more and more beautiful just ahead of us opening our doors. I remembered that both our spirits were lifted when the streets warmed, the flowers bloomed, the birds sang, and the water at the bay became so clean, clear, and inviting. It was like Mother Nature had decided to give us a real shot in the arm, and played the perfect host, laying on the most inspirational display to see if we could make this thing work.

The very first of our many guests that year were not disappointed, even if the management of *The Admiral* had got itself confused by their arrival time. They settled in well, went off to Krka National Park, to Split, to Šibenik, and rested deeply at our little retreat all the way through.

Niko and Andrea could not have been better staff , or have been more graceful and charming. We could not have been prouder of our team.

Before our inaugural visitors set off back to the States, they asked what we missed most about home, about daily life in California. We said we thought often about the insane choices of food, mostly about the rich aromas and explosive flavors of high-quality tacos. A couple of weeks later they wrote a really cool review on *Booking.com*. The first ever written about our hotel. And soon after a package arrived. Inside was a tortilla press, flour, and ranch dressing.

The bookings stacked up fast, quicker than expected, and we were headed towards a full house by early July. We actually only finished the decorating in June, the last touches being put in place by our favorite Californian illustrator Priscilla C. Witte. She flew over for a few days, traveled around, marinated herself in Dalmatian scenes and culture a little before creating the image of *The Admiral* himself, a nautical character.

He was brought to life in a ceiling mural and his huge presence added inescapable character to the bar. We put some of her paintings around the hotel too, nautical themes, really cool fresh toned designs that tied everything together.

People had been reacting fantastically to the digital images we had been supplying, and had seen them worldwide in magazines, newspapers, and online. People who were tracking our remodeling progress on Facebook and Instagram were booking in, playing an active, important part in a story they had followed for a while. When prospective guests looked us up, they found, not just the new story of the old hotel, but also the story of us, the young Americans who fell in love with Croatia.

Some said they admired the journey we were on, respected it, talked about how they had thought of doing something like that too but never had the chance, the money, or the balls. It was a welcome reminder of the big leap we took. Some even took selfies with us and said things like, "People must have said you were nuts!"

We could only answer, "They sure did."

We took on a lawyer in Šibenik and asked her to get some background on the hotel. It felt like we were being overcautious in doing that, but we sunk not just all our money into everything but also so much of ourselves. It was like our DNA was in the walls and floors of the building. It would have been foolish not to do our best to make sure we knew of any danger on the horizon.

At the outset, Karlo's books hadn't made sense. We'd been shown documentation back when we were considering purchasing the place and it was crystal clear the hotel wasn't making money. But was that the full story? Our instincts at that point told us to move forward with caution, and all things considered, that was one reason we chose to rent for three seasons instead of buying it at the €1.5M asking price. We considered that sum to be a little overenthusiastic. Besides, it was out of our reach.

Our landlord's behavior since then seemed a little random, even negative in places. We felt he had interfered unnecessarily, and been less involved at the more important times. Verbal commitments had not worked out, assurances and promises had been ditched or delayed.

We felt after our initial agreement to rent that the contract we put in place needed to be rock solid. At one stage, early on, we tried to get a notary to help us make the paperwork more formal. But some issues emerged in terms of the background of the hotel's ownership and us being foreigners. It all slowed things down at a time when we needed to get moving.

The lawyer we engaged to comb through everything started by digging out every document she could on the place, all land registry data for *La Perla* going right back to its inception in 1950. While everything seemed above board at first sight, she matched what the notary had said when she explained that recent details were unclear. She told us some of the information didn't make sense.

Karlo, she said, initially owned the hotel together with a previous business partner. That partner, we came to know, cleared out of Croatia and was last known to be living in Panama. Seemed he basically left Karlo high and dry and a lot of loans got tied to the building. The mysterious disappearing man owed money but chose to split.

With our business cranking up a gear as the tourists arrived, and with our heads already choc-a-bloc with the things we needed to get done yesterday, we asked the lawyer to dumb it all down for us, to say what this meant for us.

She said there were no immediate answers but that it would take time to get everything investigated, cross-referenced, and straightened out. She said if we wanted a notary to come in and attest to everything, we would have to be patient because important questions needed answers.

We felt this was worth raising with Karlo and some of the business agents who worked with him. A man from Karlo's office got in touch. He made reference to the Panama situation and said that issue should not affect our relationship with Karlo in any way. He said he would see what he could do to clean this all up. He got back in touch to say there was a notary who understood the situation, who could clear this all up for us. That would mean we could move on with tightening up arrangements, which would be to everyone's benefit.

We spoke to our lawyer and told her we didn't have time to sit around feeling insecure. That we were happy to just get this over and done with. She said she would prefer to do this her way. We told her we had to adapt to the circumstances and that the notary was registered and above board.

Besides, as the hotel was looking great, as the tourists were book-ing in, and as we got the impression we were getting along better with Karlo, we were not too keen on getting too deeply involved in any unnecessary legal background stuff. We felt that getting the contract opened up ahead of a rework would allow us to press for the rent to be lowered. From our point of view, we needed to be sure about the deal as it impacted on our lease. We didn't give a shit about a shady man in Panama.

We wrote to Karlo and asked for a rent reduction as long as we kept things simple.

There was a lot going on in our lives. We were getting run off our feet. Barely getting time to eat. Trying to work with the Croatian language. Trying to keep the departing guests happy. The current guests happy. Arriving guests happy. Bar customers happy. Trying to take on staff for cleaning and bar duties. Trying to keep each other functioning as well as we could. Watching every penny coming in and going out.

One mistake we made was to allow people to book in for just one night. It meant we had those all-important arrival and departure interactions within a short space of time, and rooms had to be turned around rapidly every day. Within a week or so we realized why so many hotels in tourist areas have a two-night minimum or more, but it was too late by then. Our books were too full and our one-night stays were too popular. Folks who were touring Europe or trekking Croatia were already stopping by for the night. Many had heard about a cool new boutique hotel. They could check out our story, our photography and footage online, and when they did, the value of how we pitched our product really showed itself.

We were young hoteliers who caught the wave from an unprecedented tourism swell in Croatia, working in an industry that was supercharged by social media. We knew the power of imagery, of the promise of experience as an appeal point as much as we knew that reputation would maintain what we had started. We set out to inspire image literate people through the various platforms and it was really working.

This was a time of increasing flight numbers and historically low airfares all across Europe. More and more people around the world were seeking to vacation off the beaten track, to replace the names of well-known nations and cities with words that were not so familiar to them. The reworked four floors of a fifties socialist meeting house on the island-rich Adriatic coast sounded appealing to westerners.

It all meant guests were more likely to interact with Megan and I online, to like and comment on our updates, and most significantly, to confirm their place in the story by leaving reviews. So many great words were written by often excited people, freshly back from a new place and new adventure, their cellphones filled with the best pictures they had ever taken.

By midsummer 2016 in Zaton, we had everything a new generation of open-minded tourists could want. Sure, we had no restaurant, but *Porat* next door was authentic, quality, reasonable, and friendly. We had issues with the electricity and got hit by power cuts that impacted the whole region, but with a little patience, good humor, and the help of Romeo, we got through just fine.

Across all of that whole hectic season, beyond a couple of gripes that we did not have a sports channel dedicated to soccer (which we promised to address), and that we double booked a few rooms (damn that booking system... yet we always got them a bed in the end), we had no complaints.

When one or the other of us got away from reception, maybe to take on some cleaning or serving or a little staff training or to check what a word meant or rescue someone from Sailor or do some laundry gathering or some bar stocking, we would get called back all the time. Andrea, usually, or Niko, would shout out or send a message asking for one of us to come and speak to some arriving or departing guests.

The guests could be from the US, the UK, from France or Germany or Sweden or Russia and they would introduce themselves, say they liked our story, tell us how they had seen some brilliant pictures online, that everything was as gorgeous as the images suggested it would be, and ask us all about it.

That side of things started to eat up time, and as we looked at the schedule for each working day, we began factoring in the hours we would need to spend having coffee or beer with guests while talking about our time in Croatia, discussing the remodel, explaining how a couple would leave California to come to Croatia to renovate an old hotel.

I would be collecting fruit and Andrea's text would come in.

Sorry, *they don't want to talk to local people so you have to come now.*

Or Megan would be sweeping the terrace and Andrea would say, "Sorry, but they say they want to meet you because they read about you."

Sometimes guests just wanted to hang out with us. Much as we loved having them and much as we appreciated the idea we were some kind of draw ourselves, we found it was eating up precious time.

But we were as much a part of the place as the new floors and cushions, as the new boho bar tiles and weirdly patchy bed linen.

After a few weeks it felt like the outworking of our initial burst of success was something we would have to address.

But we did go far with all of that. We did have dinner with people and paid for their food and drinks, because it felt like the right thing to do. It was like we didn't want to disappoint anyone, didn't want to give any impression that we did not truly appreciate the presence of every single guest in *The Admiral*.

We did what we could every day until we decided we were reaching an end, that we would have to set boundaries. We were working eighty and ninety hour weeks just to keep things at the basic standard and we could not go on like that. Towards the end of the first season, we were going crazy.

(Megan)

I had to take a lead on entertaining guests because Jonathan doesn't like to say no to people. He really doesn't mind an open-ended conversation with a random person even when there are other things to do. Generally speaking, I was more about the guest relations with our visitors, he was more like a fellow guest.

We were both happy to spend a little while with guests but it really did start to become like we were taking time with some and avoiding others.

We would tell each other how the rent was killing us, that we would be way better off if we tightened things up at the hotel, gifted ourselves a little more time for each other, more time to enjoy our new country.

We wrote again to Karlo to explain the situation and said that we had played fair with him. We said he must know how well we were making it work but said we were still really feeling the squeeze, asked him and his agents again to cut us some slack, and there was always resistance or excuses in return.

And in the hotel we began saying to guests, "We're so sorry, we can't do that..." and saying, "You know, we'll get a drink with you but we've so much to do..." We used the greatest diplomacy to ensure people would not go away annoyed or frustrated and write something harsh and break that chain of great reviews.

(Jonathan)

I GOT the boat in July and I guess, as a guy who grew up with boats in Orange County, who missed getting onto the water, that was one of the best moments of my year.

It took a while to figure it all out and get everything working as it should. The engine, the rules, the red tape, the docking, fueling... all of those things were different.

My plan had always been to have lots of boat trips to the islands, to have morning trips, sunset trips, little coastal tours here and there, loosely structured away days.

It was a rigid inflatable, one of those fast boats like the military uses. I knew it would be the perfect size for our needs. It could hold eight guests and yours truly, Captain Jonathan. It had no cabin, nothing like that, but was very versatile and could go anywhere within reason, as long as it had the gas. But I was going to need somewhere to dock it and a license to be its captain.

I spoke with Josip about that side of things because he knew the system and the waters better than anyone and was a fisherman himself. I figured he would be able to advise who to call or who to furnish with chocolates or cologne, or if it was needed, some used notes in a brown envelope.

He said he would help, that he understood how I wanted to get out onto the water as soon as I could, and said he figured the guests would be lining up to do the same because the tourist market for island trips had been growing for years.

We got to talking in detail about it and he said the islands were like a lifeline to him, that he could find perfect peace out there. We already knew how most of them have a little coffee shop or bar or café, a couple of little old houses or meadows just packed with astonishing color.

And we already knew what he said about the signs saying "Wi-Fi" that were very often something close to a lie, that people who were selling things on the islands saw that word as a sales point. In many cases when you get out there you find no wi-fi at all. We both could see how zero wi-fi could be a good thing.

We had been to many of the islands and found our own hotspots of happiness. We knew some hidden away cafes where the fish were no older than the sunrise and the quiet was full and deep, and a couple of bars where life felt easy. I knew pretty soon I would be able to visit the islands anytime I wanted, jump in the brig with no notice at all, head on over with Megan, Sailor, guests, whoever, whenever.

Josip said a thing he loved to do was drink when he got out there, to sink a few cold ones where the pressure was off. He said he had merrily made his way back to Zaton from the islands many times after many a long day of drinking. It sounded great.

In terms of getting me legal, the fastest way was straightforward. I needed to visit the harbormaster in Šibenik, register myself, register the boat, and I would be in business. And in terms of getting me somewhere to park the boat, he said to leave that to him.

So I arranged the earliest appointment I could get with the harbormaster, read all I could find about the rules and tides and traffic volume and showed up ready to rock. And it was just this one guy sitting there, the harbormaster himself. He had that grumpy Croatian face thing going on, and was not too happy with his day, not looking like he was delighted to meet me. I guess we both knew there might be a problem at the outset given he basically didn't speak a word of English. And all I knew in Croatian was a couple of mom jokes and *jebiga*.

He did this unusual thing I had never seen before where he cleared his desk, took out a few toy boats, and set them down. He moved them around a little, invited me to do the same, to show him how I figured I would drive the boat with other boats around, which side of the water I should take, at what speed I should be going.

I was more used to sailboats than rigid inflatables, but I tried not to let that show and did what he asked. The thing about sailboats was they have the right of way as they don't maneuver so well, so I needed a quick mindset adjustment.

At first it wasn't clear to me if his toy boats were sailboats or not, but I think I soon got the hang of it. So I was moving those little toys around his desk and he started asking me questions in a kind of a Croatian-English mish-mash. He showed me this manual. It had three hundred pages and he was dipping in, pointing, asking random questions.

I tried to answer as best I could. I mean, I knew the rules or could at least figure out any questions he might have and had a lot of experience on the water. But the circumstances of this little test meant neither of us was getting through to each other.

So we struggled for a while and I answered what I thought he was asking but his face was not getting any less annoyed and his tone wasn't getting any lighter. So he waved his hand, got me to stop talking, got me to put down his little boat. I figured he was going to throw me out, tell me to come back when I had learned Croatian or at least come back with a Croatian speaker.

That wouldn't have been totally unreasonable, but at that moment I was feeling a little bullish because I knew this stuff, I knew how traffic worked on the water. I was basically getting ready to use the F-bomb in Croatian to make a point, considering even telling him how well I knew his mom.

He said, "Go".

And we looked at each other.

I asked, "So do I...?"

He said, "Yes, yes, okay, license, yes."

I was pretty pumped. It had all happened over about five minutes, and it was five minutes well spent. I was now a captain. A lady at the desk on the way out had me sign a form and I thanked her, folded up my permit, and left for Zaton.

From there we could really begin to work on that offer to guests, design it, price it up, market boat trips as activities and excursions in the lobby and bedrooms.

But the trips would take time and would need to be booked in advance. Scheduling trips meant that any unforeseen developing issues or urgent business at the hotel could not always be a priority for all concerned. That side of it was a little uncertain. I figured pretty soon it would be crazy to take all of this on my own, but then I was the only one with a captain's license.

"Hey," I said to Josip, who knew more than I did about the islands anyway. "Do you want to help take people on boat trips?"

He shrugged. Which was his way of saying yes.

TWELVE

Croatia Journal: Zaton.
September 2016.

SAILOR really hit her stride. Our early worry, that letting her run free as other dogs did around there would mean trouble, didn't come to anything. All she did was wander, sniff her way along the harbor, and hang around the park with the kids and other dogs.

After a while, she didn't spend much time inside the hotel at all.

It had all been a big adjustment for her. She barked a lot in the early days. At the workmen, at Niko, Andrea, at anyone who opened any door into where she was. It got to the point where we had to shut her in a room or leave her upstairs when we knew people would be coming and going.

But Dalmatian people are dog people (no pun intended). And dog people are good people. Most people there seemed to understand a dog's nature and that being under orders to hook a canine onto a leash every time it stepped outside a building was over the top.

Americans could be overzealous about all of that stuff. Letting Sailor get used to the place and then, when she was ready, letting her get out and do her own thing, had worked well. Three years old, coming up on four, Sailor was adventurous enough to explore and smart enough to come back. A couple of times she slept outside for most of the night, which was both rebellious and a sign of growing confidence. The first time we went looking for her, knowing it was unusual to not see her face at night, we found her comfortably out of it on the terrace couch.

We were weirdly proud of how she handled it all. She adapted and really blended in with village life. There were people who owned one or two of Sailor's friends and they'd stop by, ask if they could take her when they were going for a walk. Some people wandered in sometimes and they didn't even know our names but knew Sailor's. They just smiled and took her off for a few hours.

It could've been a lot worse. If she had fallen into some state of dog depression after never getting used to the new smorgasbord of smells and sights, and had never gotten over the loss of so much she had known so well, it would have been shit for her and shit for us.

The nagging concern we had thought was that she'd break off in the wrong direction when she was out on one of her walks, or that she'd get the zoomies and shoot into the horizon, a rebel without a leash and find herself becoming Croatia's latest landmine victim.

We were not aware of any noncombatant canines being killed by a mine there, but that's not to say it hadn't or couldn't happen. The mine clearance people were still around and we saw them often, but we could never get close enough to ask what they knew about dangers to dogs.

Some of the locals talked about the mines like they were a story of the war but not a story of the past. What they meant was that in some ways the bitter conflict there that roused such deep, burning passions even in pretty little places like Zaton, lived on in hearts and minds.

Some said the war would never be over even if no bullets were ever fired again, even if no new mines were ever slipped into the landscape. We'd seen hostility in people's faces when they saw a car with a Serbian license plate pass by, the little snarls when they talked about Serbian people. You didn't have to go far below the surface there to find raw feelings.

We had a day out with some urban explorers in the spring, some people who said they could show us some of unseen Croatia. We were thinking that could be an option in terms of an alternative tour for guests. So we drove up and trekked off to see an underground Yugoslavian Air Force base a couple of hours northeast, right on the border with Bosnia and Herzegovina.

It was built in 1948, had about five miles of subterranean tunnels, and could withstand a nuclear strike. If World War Three were to hit it's been said that a thousand people could have lasted in that place for a month or more. The Serbs tried to bomb it to rubble during the independence war. They wanted to stop the Croats from being able to use it in a move that was more symbolic than strategic. But, given a nuke wasn't enough to open its door, it was a hopeless mission.

We'd come to see the Croatian mindset and sense of national identity as being like that bunker proud and solid and unfucking breakable. This nation had been stolen and plundered and invaded and bombed and colonized a hundred times in history and you could sense it sometimes. The feeling was that there was nothing those formidable people couldn't resist or outlast. So, after getting to know the place, when the locals said the conflict of the region would never end, even if only in the headspaces of the people, you didn't doubt it.

That said, it's not just that the Croats sometimes gave the stink eye to any passing Serbs, it's that the passing Serbs often gave the stink eye right back. It's not that the Croats didn't let go of what fired them up so easily, it's that the Serbs didn't either. They were all people of the Balkans and if there was one thing they had in common it's that they were as strong-headed as bulls.

One of the real strong heads we met was Tonci, Josip's uncle. He lived in Canada for many years, and played some kind of significant role in the Balkans war before that. He owned an idyllic-looking olive grove a short drive from the back of *The Admiral*. He also knew a lot of people; knew a lot about a lot of things. It was good to meet him, to be able to talk in full English about the place. We felt we could trust him and we didn't feel like we could completely trust many people, nor that many there felt they could completely trust us.

155

We attributed that to the history and culture of the place, that there was a general suspicion of outsiders' motivations passed down through the generations. We were on the receiving end of it. But that's cool.

Tonci and some other folks asked us what we knew about the war, about the role the US played in it. They talked about how the Croatians were backed by Uncle Sam and that the people who were on the ground wouldn't forget it.

This one tiler told us how a couple of trucks rolled into little Zaton one day, a huge delivery from America. He knew the men who received some of the many weapons on board. How many? What kind? How much ammunition? Where did all the guns and grenades and rocket launchers and whatever go? No one had answers to those questions. If we had to guess, we would say that there were a lot of unregistered weapons in the homes and farms of Dalmatia.

Another story came from Tonci, who randomly said one day, "I'll tell you something you don't know."

"Okay."

He said, "That underground base you went to? It's one of the best. No one builds fortresses underground or overground like the Croatians. Go to Dubrovnik, Šibenik. Go to Kliss fortress in Split, see how it still stands solid since the Middle Ages. The *Game of Thrones* people filmed there. We can still build like that. A lot of old military Yugoslavia was designed by Croatian brains, made by Croatian muscle."

"That's very cool."

"Your country knew that fact in 1991 when it came here to deliver those weapons and show us real support."

"Cool. We didn't know that."

"No. That's not what I meant by telling you something you didn't know..."

"Okay."

"Yugoslavians built some of Saddam Hussein's underground bunkers in the 1980s, around Baghdad. One of them was modeled on one built for Marshall Tito. The concrete roof alone was fifty by ninety meters, was five meters thick, weighed five thousand tons."

He mapped out details like an expert. He told us how a conference center had been built on top of that bunker for Saddam, meaning that the center was built at ground level. He said what was underneath in terms of its depth and design was among the Iraqi dictator's best-kept secrets.

He said US backing of the Croatians included a raft of agreements struck both in corridors of power and in rooms where few knew what was said. There was a deal made, that as part of the weapons support, the people who knew their way around Hussein's bunker would talk. They were to give the Americans all the blueprints they had for all the bunkers they had worked on.

"That's what you didn't know," he said.

Unlike his uncle Tonci, Josip was not so keen on talking about history, or on talking about much at all. He enjoyed helping us put together a great cocktail list for the bar and knew that special price reduction formula that kept the locals happy.

But when it came to serving drinks to guests, he gave it a go but it wasn't for him.

He's not what you would call the most gregarious person in the world. We would describe him as being something of a classic Dalmatian, in that he loved his home, but had little interest in traveling beyond. He'd never been on a plane, had no real interest in the rest of the world, no particular interest in ever going to America, not even much interest in the rest of Croatia. He said Zagreb freaked him out because it was too far from the sea.

We would confess that, with our western mindsets, we assumed people in the former socialist east might have more interest in our homeland in the way we often have an interest in theirs. But that didn't seem to be the case. It had been uplifting to see how much people there care about the place, how much they loved their land, how precious their culture and identity were to them.

Reflecting back on the season, we knew that to local people, we were just foreigners passing through, that our control of the hotel in their village would ultimately be a temporary thing. Yet the welcome really had been starting to warm up (although it had come pretty slow at times).

One of the strangest parts of the first season had been how fast the weeks went by. It had been like pulling teeth to get to the point that we were good to go, and when the doors opened, it was intense and incredibly full-on and seemed to have raced by like lightning.

By late summer, between ourselves, Josip, Niko, Andrea, and the Porat restaurant next door, we were working hard and doing everything we could for our customers. We believed our guests were consistently happy and we really did feel like we knew why. The early indications that we would get booked up in July were right, and the same thing happened with August and it was almost as busy in September. We had been told again and again by people that they would be spreading the word about our little gem.

It seemed like most of the two or three thousand people in the area knew at least something about us and about the redevelopment of *La Perla*. This included the local mayor, Boris, who we were told had been taking an interest in our work yet we had never met him. One of our bar regulars, who liked to drop in for a seven a.m. rakija shot, told us he knew Boris, said he was usually in Šibenik but that he was surprised he hadn't been by.

One day, we asked Josip about him. If he knew Boris and what the deal was. Turned out there had been a different mayor, a whole other mayoral position in Zaton which had been held by a man called Čoga (sounds like *Choga*). Seems Čoga had friends in Zagreb, had been somehow influential in old Yugoslavia and worked with the government in ways that were never made clear.

With all the power shifts after the independence war, everything changed. The Zaton mayoral position was reshaped and was from then on to be controlled from Šibenik. A lot of people in Zaton didn't like how that turned out and didn't have all the respect for whoever took the new mayoral position they might normally have. While some were very cold towards Čoga and didn't like what he might have been associated with, others had a great deal of respect for him to this day.

He was a friend of Josip's and no friend of Boris. He still pretty much seemed to see himself as the rightful mayor of Zaton in that his term never formally came to an end. He lived behind the hotel and was in control of the private marina near *The Admiral*. It was government-owned, separated to the main city-owned marina, and had been handed over to him to run as part of his role back in the day and never taken back from him. He had all the rights and was able to sublease space to anyone he liked. That marina made lots of money.

Josip said the marina issue had been a long-running sore, that Boris wanted it back from Čoga, yet neither Boris, nor anyone else in the village, would confront him about it.

Josip arranged for Čoga to stop by to shake hands and talk about that dock. And he did so, drank an espresso in *The Admiral*, talked a little English, and we talked a little Croatian, but we decided against any mom jokes.

He was in his fifties, firm set, with strong eye contact, a man who seemed to be seeking to get the measure of us. He walked us to the water and said there would be no problem. Right then and there he gave us the use of a dock for free for as long as we needed and the use of a second one if any guests needed to park there. Josip, and now Čoga, had been useful guys to meet.

We worked it out with Josip to take the six a.m. boat trips to get the early birds up to Krka National Park to beat the rush. He would spend time with them and get back about lunchtime or so.

Krka was incredible, just beyond what you could imagine in terms of its natural beauty. It has colossal waterfalls and explosive fauna and landscapes like something from a dream or from *Game of Thrones.* People just loved to be in among all that, to hang around, to swim, to get lost in the place, and forget about the time.

Josip would come back early sometimes if people wanted to stay on longer, and then later we could arrange to go and get them. We would make snacks for them, make everything flow easily as they did their own thing. Then sometimes Josip would not come back when we expected him, but return later with the guests after their day out took a diversion. On pretty much every one of those occasions he would have had a few drinks. But as long as the guests were happy and alive and the boat hadn't crashed or sank, it was all good.

We put on a sunset cruise too. A boat trip with cocktails for people to enjoy a slow ride up the river as the sky turned blood orange over Zaton bay.

The village got way busier in the summer, as did many parts of Croatia. The country had been capturing the imagination of people around the world and the tourist numbers were climbing higher and higher. In July and August, Krka in particular was extremely busy. What was great was that we could get there fast and early via the waterway. It was like we had a hack for our guests.

The insight we were getting into all these things from our quality Croatian friends was making it all work so well. Those tourists were having a great time for sure, but sometimes when things all just worked well we figured no one could be having a greater time than us.

It was really good to meet an English-speaking couple, Dani and Ante, who lived in the village. Josip introduced us. They had parents from Zaton but had lived for a long time in Germany before taking a house there. We met up in the bar and for dinners in Split and Šibenik. We talked about getting away together for Christmas.

It turned out that Dani was a great singer, had sung in some tourist bars and restaurants in the cities, and that she has this really smooth, jazzy, bluesy thing going on with her voice. We told her she needed to be on stage at *The Admiral* as soon as possible.

We started making plans to go home for the winter. We figured we'd fly back to America for a few weeks, early October time. We needed to book flights, make sure the airline would take Sailor, make all the arrangements we needed in terms of mothballing *The Admiral*.

The hotel's bookings across the season had been good, but set against our outlay, were pretty meaningless. That's how it was going to be for a while, but we'd get there. Anyway, we were not exactly in it to make millions. We were actually waiting now on the reworked contract before we paid the next rent installment. We also would've appreciated a conversation with Karlo or one of his people which included some recognition of what had taken place across a truly great first season.

His hotel had been transformed, and had brought scores of tourists into Zaton, yet it was clear he didn't really want to talk about any of that. Seemed to us that people who were afraid of any kind of change just preferred to move along at a glacial pace.

Jebiga.

We weren't going to go running to him. He stepped into the background and it suited us best for him to stay there. We did hear things about his business dealings, rumors about the future of *The Admiral*, but nothing we could ever be sure about. We did hear on the tangled grapevines around Zaton that we might get a couple of months rent free over the winter when the hotel was closed for the off season until we opened again in April. We hoped that was right.

That year had pushed us hard but we somehow held our nerve and landed on some amazing plateau of happiness and satisfaction. The greatest feeling was not that we couldn't wait to get home, it's that we couldn't wait to get back. It really did feel that if we just held onto each other, everything would be alright.

THIRTEEN

WE let business talk slide on that journey home, decided we could help ourselves out by avoiding the subject for a while.

We could hardly believe we had so much space ahead and were looking forward to having a rest, physical and mental.

It was fun working out how much Croatian we had learned, yet it wasn't so easy to calibrate. The thing was, we could in many cases understand what was being said to us in Croatian, and could get through conversations in a stumbling, broken yet workable way. But it was harder for us to use Croatian words ourselves, especially to Croatians.

Even if we did get the pronunciation right, even if we did come close to getting the tense right, it would invite the other person to say more to us in Croatian. And that would only make things more complex. We agreed we would take in-depth lessons and try to get the hang of it in season two.

(Megan)

I GUESS it felt like Jonathan and I were decompressing on the way back to the US. I would spend Thanksgiving with my family and, thanks to an invite from Jonathan's family to their annual getaway, I would get to spend Christmas in Hawaii. After that, we decided we would take a vacation with our Croatian pals Dani and Ante in the new year. They were thinking of Thailand and we couldn't resist.

We were tired but excited, a little emotional, a bit overwrought, but we had many stories to tell and a lot of catching up to do.

I said to Jonathan, "I can't wait to be home but part of me is already looking forward to the next season."

He said, "I feel the same. We have a job to finish out there."

We talked about how the warm breeze off the bay had been turning cold again, that we wouldn't miss the winter freeze destined for Zaton. We talked about some of the land there, about the vivid wildness of the fields and olive groves beyond the back of our hotel, of the islands, of the things we wouldn't see for a while.

I wanted to reveal those places and things to people back home, to friends and family, more than just describe them or show them in images. I wanted people to really get a feel for why we went there, to be able to explain to them in the best way how it stole our hearts, how we now knew we had been right to follow our instincts.

I had more reason than ever at that point to love where we were making our lives. I had gotten to know this partner of mine so very well, to know the deepest workings of his mind, to see what it was that fired his imagination and what it was he saw, what he felt. As we faced our problems together with our tiny Team USA in Zaton, we found it easy to learn from and love each other. We found it easier to stay cool and level headed because we knew whatever happened, we had each other, that we balanced each other out so well.

We landed in Maui, got off the plane, and my sister called. She was ecstatic. She said her boyfriend asked her to marry him. I was like, *Wow!* That was some big and brilliant news for our family. I hugged Jonathan and said I wished I could hug my sister too. We raised a glass to celebrate.

Jonathan was pretty grumpy at the time. I remember the hug didn't last and that he wasn't crazy about celebrating. I knew he'd been finding it harder to switch off than I did. He was still thinking too much about things in Croatia, about getting back there, working hard again, cementing our success. He had been thinking that it would be so easy to fall back and fail.

I knew he couldn't stop thinking about the messy legal background of our hotel, talk of that much needed rent reduction confusing information that can get stuck on a loop in your mind. I asked him about it but he said it was nothing, that there was nothing to worry about.

We got some sleep, rested well, ate well, told our stories, laughed like hell with Jonathan's friends and family and had a great Christmas.

We broke away a couple of days later when he took me to meet some old Cali pals. It was not what you might think a typical Hawaiian day out might look like. It was warm enough for shorts but it was pouring down rain, teeming down all over the island.

We got into the rental and drove to the Ritz Carlton. The plan was to meet them by the beach but no one was around when we arrived. We put that down to the weather. Jonathan said they would be along, so we grabbed a Starbucks, and took a moment to appreciate the place. A surfer's paradise among surfer's paradises.

We took a stroll, felt the rain fade, felt the sun pour down, and watched as the water began to sparkle. Jonathan couldn't stop beaming and it made me laugh. He had his camera. Said he wanted to get some pictures and began taking a few shots as we walked on the warm wet sand and collected our thoughts, pulled some good air into our lungs, and got surrounded by the rhythmic roll of the mighty Pacific.

We walked for maybe thirty minutes saying little, occasionally looking at each other, smiling. Jonathan asked me to put the coffee cup down, said he wanted to get a couple of pictures of me. I put it down and when I looked back he had dropped to one knee.

And then said the words, "Will you marry me?"

I guess it's in moments like that when a girl's composure can get a little lost. I reached out and shoved him and said, "No way! Oh my God are you serious!"

He was totally serious. And I was totally saying *Yes!* A friend of his was there, hidden in the bushes, and taking shots of the moment. A helicopter was waiting too, ready to take us into the Hawaiian sky to celebrate. Jonathan had arranged a sunset cruise for later in the day.

Wow!

We talked later about our future, about what we could make of the years ahead, and talked again with yet more purpose about settling down forever in Croatia. We discussed when we would get married, both knowing that in all the places in the whole world we wanted to do it in Zaton, that we wanted our adopted home to be at the heart of all that lay in front of us.

I suggested we get married in the olive grove and that we could set up a tent in Tonci's land just beyond Zaton because my heart said there was nowhere more perfect. The olive grove was set a few miles inland from the village and had well over a hundred mature trees with nothing surrounding it, but more olive fields and hills. It was truly a magical setting.

We talked about going back, about a bigger and better second season, about some straight talking with Karlo, about looking into buying the hotel once again.

We met another couple on that Hawaiian sunset cruise. We had drinks together and talked about the realisation of our dream, about hard, brilliant days in a country they had barely heard of, how we looked forward to so many more.

Part of me was thinking the last thing they wanted to hear was another couple's time in Europe, but they really tuned in. We showed them pictures of Dalmatia, of the islands, of the hotel, and they said they would come and see it. A months later, they got back to us to say they had booked a week at *The Admiral* and could not wait. It reminded us how proud we should feel of our home. It was like we carried it with us wherever we went.

I asked Jonathan that night, when he was in better spirits about everything, what had been on his mind, why he had seemed a little down when we arrived in Hawaii. I asked if it was because he was worried about what I might say when he asked me to be his wife.

He laughed and said, "What? No. Shit. I knew you would say yes."

I shoved him again, saying I only said "Yes" as a joke. I said I couldn't wait to ditch him and get back to the traffic of L.A., get back to the assholes on Tinder, say goodbye to the great thing we were making.

He laughed again saying, "When you said your sister had just got engaged it felt like it took something away from my proposal. I just wanted everything to be right. Sorry. I was overthinking it!"

I told him he had no idea how amazing it was for two close sisters to get proposed to within the same few days, that the timing was perfect, that everything was right.

He said, "Hey, I've been doing some reading."

I was interested.

He said, "Did you know that the smallest town in the world is in Croatia?"

"Nice fact! I did not know that."

"Yep." he said. "It's called Hum. Has about thirty people."

"You wanna go?"

"Maybe one day."

"Me neither," I said. "Here's a fact for you. Did you know the Croatian national costume for women is the only one in Europe that sits above the knee?"

"Great fact! I didn't know that."

"Yep," I said. "And that's what I'm wearing for my wedding."

He said, "That's cool. Then I'm wearing the men's national costume."

"And what's that?"

"Fannypack and sweats."

"Nice."

FOURTEEN

(Jonathan)

MEGAN felt overindulged in America and that made sense to me. I guess it wasn't something we had expected. We had so much to do before launching into our second season that it wasn't easy to let it fall away from our minds. After a while of lounging around in Hawaii and California, we felt oversaturated, a little lazy.

We had gotten used to being on the go all the time, to working every single day, to life in a small village where the unforeseen was standard, where power outages and dawn alarm calls and intense fatigue were normal. Suddenly everything was switched on all the time, everything was working, everything was being pushed right at us and nothing was expected of us.

In southern California you can get anything you want. Everywhere we went we were hyper aware how our eyes and ears and heads were being filled with all these choices for things we didn't need. So much stuff, so many people, so much happening - eat, drink, buy, relax, spend.

But the clean, honest, simple family get togethers away from the non stop noise of L.A. were the best. Megan's parents at the time were living around forty-five minutes from where my dad lived so it was easy to get around and see everyone, spend time with the people who were most important to us.

After we returned from Hawaii, we had a second engagement party at her folks' place. Megan went shopping with her mom and grandma to get a wedding dress, but I wasn't supposed to know.

We started talking about our plans, about the changes we needed to make, things we needed to put in place back in Zaton to create the smoothest, greatest experience we could for everyone who came to stay.

Our second season would see the launch of our restaurant. There was a ton of stuff to do in terms of the kitchen, chefs, other staff, the menu, sourcing ingredients, promotion. Our workload was going to get heavier.

I don't think we really told anyone everything about our landlord and the situation we were dealing with in terms of the bullshit around the contract, the rent, the dishonest workers who were sent our way, the fact we felt like we could only talk in whispers sometimes. I think my dad and Megan's parents knew we had some kind of insecurity about it all, but the details were ours to handle.

Many people had been following our journey on Instagram and the more we were asked about it, the more we wanted to get back to it no matter what complications there were.

In January, we went on vacation with Dani and Ante in Thailand. Taking that time out was good. We used it as a chance to really begin planning for nine months of hard work. And we really got to appreciate how Dani was such an amazing singer, that her voice and our Friday nights were a perfect match.

They asked us if, during our time in California, we had considered staying and not going back to Croatia, if we had figured we had gone far enough with *The Admiral* and felt like walking away.

We told them the absolute truth. No, we had not. We said there was no doubt in our minds we needed to get back to it.

Moving into the 2017 season, we spent time looking at promotional ideas, how the bookings were working out, seeing if we could spark some more online excitement about the season ahead. We didn't have many reservations at the time and knew we needed to get things moving pretty fast because people made summer plans early in the year.

Guests booking in for dates during spring and summer 2017 would be able to use the new restaurant, the new California Croatia fusion concept we were calling *Konoba Kalifornija,* which roughly translated to Restaurant California. But how much could we say about that in our pitch when all we knew of it was its name, and a few rough menu ideas which included fish tacos and avocado topped pizza.

Our landlord had signed off on an updated contract, a minor rent reduction with a couple of addendums. It came down to him reducing the amount he charged for the winter months when the hotel was empty. It was enough for us to accept him being a difficult landlord for the time being, since it allowed us to get on with doing what we wanted to do.

One of the key things on our list was to recruit a chef, or maybe two. We figured that even if the stove was not the greatest around we could still try to ensure the food was. We were looking at our bistro idea, nothing too expensive, aiming to create dishes that had a classy simplicity, a fresh, easy, consistent quality that would go down well.

We reached out in Zaton and Šibenik and a few people got in touch. We lined up interviews for February and mapped out our idea for the California Croatian fusion concept in those conversations, saying we thought it could be a hit with tourists. And we got a few strange looks, spent a few silent moments waiting for potential employees to see our vision in the way we did.

Some candidates were inventive, industrious, ambitious, yet few got the overall picture. Some were used to doing the same thing over and over because they knew what sold both to tourists and locals. Some said that what we seemed to be looking for was chefs to help engineer a new culinary theory and, with honesty that we appreciated, they wondered if we had thought it through. Would this food be the kind people would want to eat more than once?

Luckily, a few liked the idea of working with us, of exploring and refining some of our ideas. We told them that, of course, they would have the right to ditch the ones they didn't think would work. And that brought some relief. In the end, we took on two local chefs and began trying things out. A few discussions followed when basically one or the other chef turned to us to say, "This is really not going to work."

One of the early plans was to have no pizza on the menu, given the whole of Croatia was already well catered for. We wanted to be a quality alternative in terms of a meal out in Zaton.

But, we stepped back from that. We were reminded that as long as everything else was good in our little restaurant, as long as it was all well made with great fresh, local ingredients, then that could complement the pizza. And it was the pizza that might well bring people to us in the first place.

So we backed off from that and hired a pizza chef named Geza. We were so pleased and listened to her. Geza made the best pizza in Dalmatia, probably the best anywhere.

She was known as 'Big Momma' in the village. Big Momma was a soft speaking yet straight talking, wonderfully demure older, larger lady. I guess in all our life experience to that point we had met very few human beings as kind and sweet as Geza. She had problems she was dealing with at home and had trouble sleeping too. Yet she proved utterly reliable, totally forgiving, and incredibly hardworking. We both loved her from the moment we met her. And, when she served up a little pizza, we were hooked.

Good pizza, she told us, was something local people would pay for and would really appreciate. She said if we put quality pizza on the menu, we would be assured of local footfall. And guests would buy pizza too. Even if the other more experimental dishes didn't move as fast, we could rely on her pizza.

So a good mix of ideas went into drawing up the menu. The pizzas, we agreed, would be a little bit different from the traditional. When it all started making its way to the mouths of our customers, local and not so local, the hits turned out to be barbecue chicken pizza (unique to the area), fresh fish tacos, bacon wrapped dates, Caesar salad, tuna salad, and burgers.

In fact, the fish tacos were pretty much the only typical, well known Californian dish on the menu, but technically speaking, that was fusion enough for us.

We also reworked the bar offerings in that second season. Josip had helped out on and off the year before, but he wasn't a natural in terms of interacting with guests. For a while Marco, a great bartender from Zagreb, had taken over and moved to the village with his girlfriend, Ana to join us. Ana helped out in the hotel, but by the second season we had to think harder about getting more permanent staff on the books.

Josip remained close during that time and had become what you might call the hotel's handyman. Anything that went wrong in the building, any problems we had, any issues with the boat, Josip would resolve them. He was green fingered too and planted a little vegetable garden patch at the back of the hotel, growing fresh food for the kitchen. His connections, his English speaking uncle Tonci, and his friendship with the influential Čoga, had already proved useful to us.

When we felt our attack plan for the season was forming well, we took that ten-minute drive to Tonci's olive grove beyond the back of our hotel. This was where Megan wanted to marry me. It was where I wanted to marry Megan. We thought nothing would get in our way.

We didn't know it at the time, but revelations about the hotel were about to change everything.

FIFTEEN

(Megan)

JONATHAN and I were married on September 9, 2017. We settled on the date early, worked out how we were going to do it all.

Word started spreading around, and it became beautiful.

People of the village would literally stop by to congratulate us. Many of them were people we had never met, who had never been in the hotel before. Total strangers would shake our hands, hug us, and say they were delighted we were tying the knot in Dalmatia. They said they hoped the sun would shine on the day and that the years ahead would be happier than we could ever imagine.

One guest, Filip, had grown up in the village and made a life in business in Belgium. He stayed with us for a time in our first and second seasons and said it always made him feel good to come home. We said that, as outsiders, it was good to see local people responding so positively to the good news of others.

In a country where tradition was still very important, and in an area where life's big occasions - weddings, births, funerals - were seen as priceless punctuation marks for, not just families, but whole communities, it was as if our engagement opened doors. It brought us closer to the warm heart of the little village that was now our home too.

The closer we got to our big day, the more people would stop by with their well-wishes, with wonderful gifts, with stories of their own marriage, with questions about plans we might have for children, about how many we wanted, how many boys, how many girls. It happened over and over. It was sincere and tender, and in its own little way, told the story of the people of Zaton.

Tonci's land was confirmed as the venue after we explained how it stirred us on our first visit. It was, to be clear, basically a chunk of farm between two villages, but to our minds it was picture postcard Croatia, the ideal setting for our most important day. We both wanted something intimate and could imagine a small crowd gathered in celebration in the huge spread of the ancient olive grove.

Jonathan captured the location on camera in all its wild glory when we first visited. We would both later tell each other how we thought it would make a perfect venue for our marriage before we even spoke of taking that step.

Our hotel was ten minutes away from the grove, right next to the white stone Church of St Roko. We had seen beaming brides and grinning grooms come out of the church many times over recent months, heard the cheers and whoops of well-dressed family and friends. We had often clapped along, often welcomed groups from those wedding parties to our terrace just a few steps away. In all that time, we had both been thinking we might one day give our friends and family a day out too.

We advised relatives and friends as early as we could, yet said that no one should feel under any pressure to come all that way. We intended to have a celebration party when we returned to the US after our honeymoon anyway. Of course, I knew my grandparents would not be able to come so it was really important that we had that second event on home ground.

We talked it all over and hired a wedding planner from Zagreb to help arrange everything. So much needed to be done in terms of holding a wedding in a place without so much as running water. I mean, it was a field, right? All the issues of seating, the cake, the catering, parking, walkways, access, flowers, photography, electricity, music, toilets, the service itself, were just too much for us to take on as the rooms of our hotel filled once more across July and August.

Our wedding planner was an Australian-Croatian, a brilliant help to us, knew all the right people, knew how to kick ass when needed. Without her, we wouldn't have known where to start. So few of the companies we used for any of those services had an online presence let alone online reviews, so her insight into everything around an event as important to us as our wedding was invaluable.

I would never forget how she helped out when my wedding dress got held up in customs. I bought it with my mom and grandma in San Diego. After alterations, it was sent to me but got held up for a month.

I couldn't make sense of it and was pretty much at the point of tearing my hair out. Customs wanted me to pay all these taxes which came very close to the cost of the dress itself. It seemed irrational, like they had picked a random number and wanted me to pay it. Anyway, our wedding planner contacted somebody and it was released the next day.

Around fifteen guests from the village were invited, while about forty would be flying in from the US. All would be witnessing us saying "I do," yet for the Americans, it would be their first time seeing our gorgeous tiny town in real life. As a couple who had changed our lives to chase a dream, there could be no more significant occasion than our wedding day in Zaton.

Most guests arrived a week before and booked rooms in our fine little boutique hotel called *The Admiral*. Five houses in the village were rented out too.

Our staff were extraordinary across all of this. As the day came into view, Niko and Andrea and Geza and the others pressed upon us that we must step back, saying we should have zero concerns in our minds.

If only that could have been the case.

That summer we got some news about the hotel. It shook us. We learned that the hotel was to be sold. It would go up for auction on a date that was yet to be decided. All of this had been arranged behind our backs, over our heads, out of sight.

Unbeknown to us, our landlord had used the property as collateral to secure a loan years before we had come along. Now it seemed he had defaulted on this loan and the bank was now in control of the future of *The Admiral*.

Maybe it was the emotion of the time, maybe it was because we had come so far, had been moving forward so well, maybe because we were on the verge of becoming a married couple, but the news was a hammer blow. It felt like a betrayal, that we had been purposefully kept in the dark. In all this time we had been building something that was only ever available for rent until the bank got around to selling it to recoup the debt. We were little more than placeholders in a bigger picture.

We had always been clear with Karlo that we remained interested in buying the place and had signed that lease for three years to see if we liked life in Croatia.

What was going under the hammer wasn't just Karlo's building, it was what we had made of it. The restaurant was in business, the rooms were full, locals were regulars in the bar, guests from around the world were writing amazing reviews, and we were finally making a profit.

Everything good happening at *The Admiral* was down to us and our work, and now our creation would be used to secure the highest price for the bank as a result of someone else's debt.

It was right at this point too that we had press trips arranged – influential journalists had been invited to see the beauty of the region, stopping off as our guests. But what of all that now? It was infuriating.

We made contact with Karlo and people he worked with, asked Niko and Andrea, but each time we were told nothing was changing, that our lease remained in place.

As the end of the season approached, as our wedding day drew near, more solid truths began to emerge. There had been an auction before, right at the point when we were signing up for our first season the previous year, but there had been no bidders.

We eventually got to know about the new auction because as sitting tenants we had to be informed by law. The building was listed with the court as being for sale and a letter arrived advising us to act accordingly.

Part of the anguish was that we didn't know what this would mean. Would the sale pull apart the updated rent reduction deal we had signed with Karlo ahead of the second season? Would the rent go up after the place was sold? Would we, could we, be booted out of our home?

By the time our wedding day came, we had a date for the auction.

It would take place in four weeks.

I had never felt so insecure, right at a time when I should have been feeling the opposite. Jonathan was a mess, wasn't sleeping, was angry, depressed. And I was lying awake at night too, feeling so vulnerable right after being buoyed up with a wonderful combination of love and hope.

We talked about how exposed and weak this could leave us at a time when we were already funding an expensive wedding, when the hundreds of thousands we had already put into the hotel was still being paid off.

We got in touch with lawyers, got someone to find out exactly what our position was in the hope we could get at least some peace of mind.

In that period, as our heads filled with confusion and anger, we relied heavily on each other to get through, to at least have the greatest wedding day we could, to not let them take that from us. But we could not, would not, ever forgive Karlo for the cruel position he put us in at that point in our lives, for keeping us in the dark about everything from the start.

Before we married, we talked of the things in our lives that were good, all the things we loved. We could not pretend those things did not include our lives as they were, our hotel as we had created it.

We would have to fight for it.

"We'll buy it," said Jonathan.

"What with?" I asked.

"We'll find a way," he said.

Buying the property had been the plan of course.

But now?

(Jonathan)

MEGAN and I sat out on the terrace one evening in late summer with Josip and some others, looking out at the bay, talking about how we couldn't bear to lose what we had there. I was feeling pretty shitty, pretty blue.

Josip tried to lift my spirits. We were having this broken English-Croatian conversation and he was advising me of some good expressions, some real *fuck yous* I could maybe use next time I saw Karlo.

One guy who I didn't know was there, a local man. He told me a lot of people weren't exactly keen on Karlo having ever owned the old building, that people didn't like him in Zaton. This stranger, Ivan, said he had experience with the auction system. He said, as with many other processes in his country, there were ways that people could stack the odds against us, even at an auction. If the seller, for example, was determined to sell to someone specific or a particular buyer was determined to win at all costs, there had been cases where that could be arranged.

I was interested to hear more. We felt like we were being rail roaded so maybe it was time we played hardball too. I asked this guy Ivan to spell it out.

He said the auction would ultimately be the responsibility of a judge. That it was possible to find out in advance who that judge would be. He also said it was possible that if we were to secure the support of that judge, then he might help us find or even create holes in the process that could guide the hotel into our hands.

I didn't give a shit about the rights and wrongs of something like that anymore. I told Ivan we would do whatever it took. He said to let him look into it. I said, "Sure."

We began registering our interest anyway and had to make a €100,000 {$117,000} down payment in court just to take part in the auction. On the day we handed over the money we were aware that things could get even worse.

(Megan)

MY younger sister Tara was my maid of honor. My good friend from college, Stacy, my best friend from childhood, Kate, and my and Jonathan's mutual friend, Alexis, were my bridesmaids.

Jonathan had both of his brothers, Brian and Stone, as best men. His friend, Daniel, who he grew up with, another friend, Adam, from college, and Ante were his groomsmen. Josip was supposed to be in the wedding party but got super nervous and ended up a low profile usher. He looked great. It was the first time we had seen him without the sweats and fanny pack. And he did smile a few times.

The tent had a clear ceiling, yet the weather turned out perfect. It had rained for a few days right up to our wedding day, and the day after, we saw a huge storm. But the day itself was just right.

A previous hotel guest, a lovely English woman named Kate, took the service. She and her partner had stayed with us earlier that season before going to a yoga retreat on one of the islands. She was a wedding celebrant in London, a really sweet, very spiritual person.

I'm from a Catholic background, Jonathan's from a Jewish background, so it was important we didn't have just the one faith represented, that it was a spiritual thing above all else. And in that lovely Jewish tradition, I stomped on the glass after we made our vows.

It had been such an amazing time for all of us. Our friends and relatives went to Krka and Šibenik, took their own time out to look around the region. And we all came together for huge meals and, of course, we each had our bachelor and bachelorette parties.

Jonathan's brother, Brian, one of the two best men, is a doctor like his father, and isn't what anyone would call an overly emotional man. Yet he shed tears as he made his speech, as did a few others in the marquee.

Brian talked of how amazing it was for everyone to be there, to be joining us in the country to where he and Jonathan had traveled as backpackers ten years before. He said there was a completion to the whole thing, that it had all been an incredible accomplishment by his little brother and had unexpectedly turned out to mean so much to the whole family.

I was crying my eyes out!

We took a moment out from the party after all that, walked down the slope from the marquee towards a little clump of trees, held onto each other for a while, talked about our number one goal being love and happiness for the rest of our lives, come what may. Right then, like some kind of magic, fireworks started going off over the olive grove, a surprise celebration lighting up the dimming sky.

It had been arranged by Tonchi's family, kept secret from us. Me and my husband stood among those trees and watched that take place and were amazed. It was so incredible it took the breath from our lungs and put tears in our eyes. We lost all our words, kissed right there, held each other tight.

We spent the next few days thanking everyone, seeing them all safely back to the airport and getting back to Zaton ahead of closing up for season's end.

Word came that the auction had been postponed for whatever reason, that it would now take place in November instead. It was good to get a little space to breathe, but we found out the sale would go ahead right when we were in Thailand, right in the middle of our honeymoon.

⟶

(Jonathan)

The delay was good but it was like a punch in the gut for Megan and I to know we wouldn't even be in Croatia when the auction took place. We would be on our honeymoon. So another important part of our lives was getting dumped on.

Our lawyer said that when our lease had changed after our landlords reduced the rent, an addendum had been drawn up which might now come into play.

As part of the payback for reducing the rent squeeze, the lease granted access to the account from which we paid our bills. The idea was if we didn't pay our bill, they could legally take money from there.

We tried to get some clarity on how that could come into play, how the lawyer had not made us aware of this earlier, on what it might mean, on what we should do, and the advice was unclear. In fact, it was all over the place.

We ditched him, got another lawyer, and asked them what was our best move. Should we raise issues about the addendum check if it was legitimate in the first place? We asked if the bank had a say in this, if all rental issues were down to Karlo even though his hotel was in the hands of the bank. Again, the advice was poor. In the end we ditched them too and got a fresh lawyer.

From our view, things were getting murkier and murkier. We had to ask one lawyer how they didn't understand what was going on.

We asked another, "Do you not know if we have any say in any of this?" We even asked, "How do we know we can trust you?" But that got us nowhere. All it did was confirm the state of our minds around that time.

At one stage, when it felt like everything was stacked against us, we asked ourselves if we were feeling paranoid about how this was all playing out. In one case, we learned that a law firm we used was also used by Karlo and we had to wonder if that company had a conflict of interest acting against us. Overall we weren't too keen on how all of this was panning out, especially with the corruption we knew was rampant throughout the country.

I got back to Ivan, the guy from the village who approached us a few weeks before at the hotel about the situation in a sort of desperation. Just to check if there was any way we could get a judge on board or if we could bribe anyone in the legal chain linked to *The Admiral*.

Could we swing things our way? We weren't the sort of people who made backroom deals, but we knew how things worked there in Croatia and in our minds it was better to play ball.

We felt like the lawyers were useless, that they couldn't work out our legal position, that they had no idea what our rights were. The contract was a mess, the addendum was confusing.

He said he couldn't help us, that we were barking up the wrong tree, that we would have to drop it now, forget he ever said he could help us.

I was like, "What the fuck?"

To this day, I don't know what his plan was or if he was full of shit in the first place. We didn't know who he really was, what his real aim was, if he was a spy for someone else, if he was out to help or hinder us from the start.

The whole thing was so dirty that Megan and I felt we had no hope, no chance, that we were going to lose, and whatever happened after that would be beyond our control.

I became convinced this would be it. That we were done, that the second season was our last, that we were about to lose the hotel, our home, our work. I was sure that all this shit would be the first thing to happen to us as a married couple.

But we had to move on with the process. I remembered so clearly that day we took ourselves to the courthouse as part of the deal to lodge €100,000 ahead of the auction. After doing what we needed to do, we grabbed a coffee in a little cafe right across the street. We saw this guy go in who looked familiar. And we watched him come out again.

We were asking each other, "Who is that guy?" We wondered how we knew his face. Then it came to us. He was a guest at our hotel. We had served him his breakfast that morning. His name was Filip, a well off, locally born businessman living in Belgium.

He had just made a deposit. He was to be the second bidder. No wonder he had enjoyed staying at *The Admiral*, enjoyed walking around, inspecting everything, taking it all in. He had every expectation he would be the new owner.

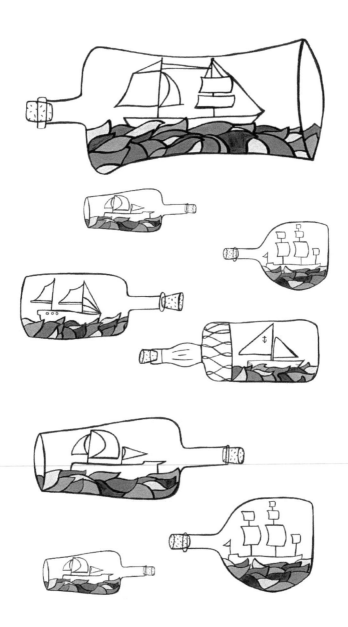

SIXTEEN

(Jonathan)

I GUESS there's no clear reason why some things stuck in the mind. Looking back, it's like my head had this thick soup of recollections, this mix of the joyful and lovely, of the hurtful and terrible. Also, there were a couple of memories that were just plain weird.

For example, I was joyful during Sveti Roko, a local festival honoring the saint of the village. A small replica cannon was pointed out into the bay while what looked like a trash can was floating in the middle of the channel as some sort of makeshift target. It got weird when I realized it wasn't a replica but an actual tiny, loaded cannon. It sparked up and smoke started pouring out the end as it was getting ready to fire out on the water. The locals cheered. And I watched as the whole contraption glided menacingly over the surface, closer, and closer to my beloved boat.

I was actually late in working out that the rinky dink thing was actually going to explode. People around me who knew the deal were watching my face as it pointed towards my boat which was docked in the harbor.

I was like, "So, what happens here?"

And there was laughter.

"Wait - is it going to fire an actual little cannonball at my boat? Oh my god, my boat!"

A lot of our Croatian experience was like that. We just weren't always sure what was going on, what was about to happen, why some things did happen. Sometimes it was bad luck, a lot of the time we were kept in the dark. Other times we were just misled. Other times we were, more or less, robbed.

Anyway, what could I do about the little cannon or the floating trash can? Not much. So I shrugged, people laughed, and there was, as everyone expected, a bang. Flames shot out and bits and pieces of something were propelled over the water and splashed all around the place. I figured if anyone had been in range it could have taken a piece out of them. But luckily none of it reached my boat. The fire just burned out.

I asked people what was going on there and never got a full answer. The festival itself was a pretty big deal each summer. It was like this roving carnival all alive with color and making its way through the whole village, booths all along the harbor. But the fact was that no one seemed to be able to explain that cannon part of it, although I didn't dig too deep. I guess it was a reenactment of some kind.

Didn't matter, anyway. As a matter of fact, I once tried to see if we could get some kind of fireworks for the Fourth of July. I thought about putting on a spectacle, doing some American cocktails. I asked around and was told I would need city approval. That would have meant visiting someone in Šibenik with more flowers and chocolates, so I just let it go. Besides, not many people knew what the Fourth of July was about.

The situation with the auction in November was way more confusing than the cannon or the flaming floating trash can. And way more distressing. The sale had been knocked back to take place when we were on our honeymoon. We had an agent bidding for us on the floor and sending updates to Megan's phone while we waited in our hotel room in Thailand.

It was tense being up against a guy who had been our guest. We knew Filip had money. And he had demonstrated his interest by staying with us at least two times, by walking around admiring the hotel while he was there.

Megan and I agreed we would put our dukes up and fight hard. We would go as far as €700,000 {$830,000}. Absolute max. We knew that figure was insane, that on paper we couldn't afford it. Yet, if we were able to secure *The Admiral* forever at that price, we felt we had the passion and grit to not let it all die. It was a figure that, in financial terms, would push us right to the most dangerous edge of the highest cliff. But I guess we were less scared of heights now, more scared of losing our dream than losing our footing.

So we had been raising money in dollars, doing a lot of our official dealing in euros and the bidding was taking place in kuna, which is the local Croatian currency. We knew it might get confusing.

On WhatsApp, right before the auction began the conversation went something like,

Agent: There is a third bidder.
Megan: How can there be a third bidder?
Megan: Do you know who it is?
Agent: There is a third bidder.
Megan: I know. How? I thought no one else could bid.
*   Who is it?*
Agent: From USA.
Megan: Seriously? This is insane.
Megan: Did you get the name?
Megan: Doesn't matter now. Sorry.
Agent: They may be from the UK.

The system was screwed. This was a closed auction, barely advertised anywhere. All bidders had to declare their hand in advance, lodge that €100,000 {$118,000} with the court. How was it that another bidder got in at the last second? When did they announce their involvement? Had they lodged their down payment? What did this all mean?

And then it began, this half-assed auction, this shady, stinking sham of an event. Megan sat at the side of our little in-room pool as the numbers started rolling in. It began at 3,000,000 kuna, about €400,000, or about $430,000. And I dropped down under the water for a few seconds. I tried not to think about the money.

So the bid started climbing fast through the hundreds of thousands, shooting on up into the millions. These people were laying out how much they wanted to spend after seeing our hotel in person or on Google. They liked the result of our efforts, and wanted it for themselves. I can't say it didn't hurt, that the arrival of every message didn't feel like a dirty punch.

And they were bidding like they meant it. Those speeding figures, our racing hearts, nervous stomachs, thumping hearts, all one colliding, confused mess.

Agent: 3,900,000.
Agent: They are Hungarian but speak Eng.
Agent: 3,920,000.
Agent: 4,250,000.
Agent: You write back when we go over.
Agent: 4,500,000.
Megan: Yes.
Agent: 4,700,000.
Megan: Who keeps bidding up?
Agent: All.
Agent: 4,800,000.
Megan: Stop at 700,000 euros.
Agent: 5,000,000.
Megan: Stop at 5,288,875 kuna (or €700,000)
Agent: Ok.

Agent: 5,220,000.
Megan: Everyone is still bidding?
Agent: 5,240,000.
Agent: Yes.
Agent: 5,270,000.
Agent: 5,280,000.
Megan: Ok we're done.
Agent: It goes on.
Agent: 5,480,000.
Agent: 5,500,000.
Agent: You still want to bid?
Agent: 5,510,000.
Megan: No.
Agent: Ok.

Our plan died just like that.

We would never own *The Admiral*, could never afford to buy it, would never go on to remodel a second *Admiral*, a third or more. I wanted to scream. And Megan fired this watermelon juice vomit all over me like her head exploded. If anyone ever asked me to list the shittiest days of my life, that one day on my honeymoon was going to be right up there.

We settled down, ordered a bottle of wine, and tried to find the bright side, which wasn't easy.

Filip had won the auction. I called him up at his home in France the next day, congratulated him, asked if we could have a conversation about his plans. He said he didn't speak English but, with the help of his son, he said he appreciated our position. He reminded me he was from the Zaton area, in his 40s, was making investments, said his parents still lived in the village, said he couldn't pass up an opportunity to buy the old meeting house.

I asked him about our future and he said everything was cool. He said he knew there was a three season contract and that our third season lay ahead in 2018. What lay beyond that, he said, was unclear and we would need to talk. And 'unclear' was just the sort of thing we did not need in our lives. I said that we had remodeled the hotel, furnished the hotel, put it on the map like it never had been before with minimal help. He said he was aware of all that, and said we would talk it over.

He also said that he was developing another property in the village, an Air BnB which he felt could use Megan's design touch when it went on the market. He wondered if we might be interested in helping with that. That actually sounded sincere to me.

Then he said he didn't want us to not like him. I figured that was perceptive because right at that point I didn't like him at all, and didn't have a good feeling about what he was saying. But there was nothing I could do. Megan told me later she had her reservations too, but she was willing to cut him a bit of slack. We didn't agree.

Our last contact with Niko and Andrea came soon after. That second season was done and we all knew they wouldn't be back for the third. It was never expressly said, but with Karlo moving out of the picture, it made sense that his family should move out too.

Karlo and his people had left us in the dark, treated us like fools, like enemies and never like actual legitimate tenants, certainly never like partners. It had all been extremely disrespectful. And when it came to money, we could talk all day about things we should not have done, about things he should have done. But that was all crazy messy. We needed to let it go.

From that point on, as Niko and Andrea were able to work out, what went on behind the scenes in *The Admiral* would no longer be any business of Karlo. We said our goodbyes. It was over.

Megan, Sailor, and I settled in as the big white winter came calling on Dalmatia. We had lost a lot of heart, lost some direction, felt a little blue in that hotel and its silent village over those cold weeks.

We talked about going home for a while, but never got to firming up the plans, never felt the need to add to the amount of money we had already spent over those months. I don't think we would have been sparkling company over the holidays anyway.

We bought a little tree, stocked up on comfort food and snacks. We made our bedroom as cozy as could be, pretty much created our own little island overlooking the bay. We watched *Elf* and *It's a Wonderful Life,* laughed at a few old TV shows we knew from childhood.

We drank a little wine, practiced our Croatian, and loved each other. We wrapped up warm for walks by the water, picked up on that faint smell of sewage once again, promised we would get serious about learning Croatian in 2018, that we would get the hang of the seven tenses and consonant chains come what may.

We made some money decisions, needing to cut back where we could. The PR account would have to go even though it seemed counterintuitive to stop driving the hotel forward when that had been working so well. Yet it was now someone else's property, someone else's investment. It was someone else's decision to take on the lease, someone else's decision whether our bills would rise or fall.

And we were by now starting to struggle and didn't know what our real position would be in a few months or even a few weeks. We didn't know how we would soon be feeling, if we might just keep on losing heart and want to pull the plug on the whole thing.

We were considering at that stage, for the very first time, that we might reach a point where it would be better to not have *The Admiral* in our lives. I guess, in among all the closeness of our connection that winter, we both went to a pretty dark place.

Some legal wrangles took off behind-the-scenes about the auction, about what went down and the legitimacy of it all. There were questions raised on our behalf and by Karlo's lawyer about some of the process. It had certainly been messy. The last-minute arrival of the mysterious Hungarian bidder was totally baffling.

That had really helped kick the numbers beyond our reach. Our lawyer said everything should be investigated. That investigation, in turn, slowed down the transfer of the deeds and left the hotel once more in a kind of legal limbo. But we knew this all boiled down to a scrap over procedure, that there was no hope left in terms of us owning the place.

I recalled that Sailor picked up on our glum mood. She was typically happy in Zaton, had made some great buddies, was free to roam and do what dogs needed to do. But as our spirits dipped, so did hers. I tried at one point to get a few pictures with her in the snow but she wasn't playful, wasn't springing around like before. Some of her friends had left Zaton for the season, while the owners of others just weren't around, and weren't calling over to the shut-down hotel anymore.

We wondered if Sailor might be lonely. We figured that now all the tourists and bustle and brightness of the summer had gone, she might be feeling down. And our attitude wasn't helping her come back up. We did not want a depressed dog on our hands.

We searched around and located some guy with puppies just like Sailor, Hungarian Vizslas. And they were actually from Hungary. It gave us a boost to drive a few hours northeast to the Hungarian border and pick up a whole new beautiful dog.

It all blew Sailor's crazy little mind, fired her up in a way we hadn't seen since the summer. It was like being busy again, all of a sudden having this new job to do, this new canine combination to manage. We called our new guy River after, I guess, the river. And because the water theme was there to stay in our lives.

We hooked up with Dani and Ante at that time too, and took some time out in Zagreb where they were spending Christmas. It turned out to be pretty important because we really got to appreciate the value of the friendship we had been building with them. We spent a while there, New Year's Eve too. We came away feeling good about things, no longer disappointed, no longer downbeat.

I remember coming back to Zaton on New Year's Day as our new dog and old dog played in the back. We had smiles on our faces and a reinvigorated sense that whatever the next year brought we would make it our mission to enjoy every day.

We agreed we would get back to work in February and would reopen the hotel for the season in March. It made sense to open in February at least for takeout, to sell some of Geza's world-class pizza. We even wanted some of that good stuff ourselves. Our chefs were still being paid over the winter months and lived locally anyway, so why not? February would be a good time to get back to things, also to start looking around for the new staff we would need, to generally prepare ourselves.

I went back up to our loft when we got in. I remember thinking about being able to adjust to whatever was thrown at us, thinking that whatever will be will be.

Megan followed up after, and said she had another fun fact for me.

"Oh yeah?" I said. "Go for it!"

"I'm pregnant."

My first thought? *I shouldn't have got that puppy.*

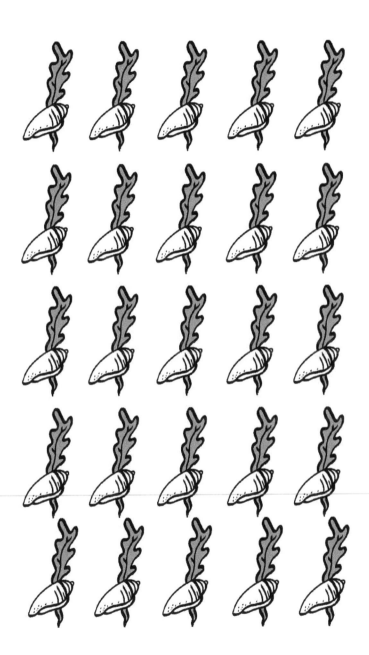

SEVENTEEN

(Megan)

MY baby bump kept growing right through the season. With perfect timing, and all being well, little Riff came in September, right after the tourists left and one year after our wedding. The opening was different this time, because our marketing hadn't been as intense. We felt disengaged for a while with everything that had been going on.

But, thanks to our great reviews, the word continued to get around and the inquiries and reservations kept coming. That said, it was still very unexpected when one major booking was made at *The Admiral* in June. It would take up a third of the rooms for the whole summer.

The reservation was for nine men from Zagreb who knew each other. They were some pretty mean looking dudes. As you would expect, all had fanny packs, pretty much all wore tank tops and shorts, most wore sandals or flip flops. They arrived over a few days in different cars, mixed among each other, had the occasional drink, were very polite, came and went at all kinds of hours. There was definitely something strange about their behavior, something that said they were not tourists.

And there was definitely something about those fanny packs. I guess we had gotten pretty proficient in the fanny pack culture of Croatia. The way these men from the fashionable urban heart of the nation had them filled out, firmly belted on, and zipped up at all times was unusual.

Jonathan and I talked to them here and there. We figured they were all colleagues, that they were not on a break, yet they were doing no obvious work.

In a short management meeting, we tried to figure out if there was something going on we should know about. We talked about those fanny packs. We had both noticed they were bulkier and heavier than usual, that whatever was in them was more than a wallet and keys, and were not just the standard sunglasses, cellphones and/or cigarette packs. Maybe the strangest thing was that the guys arranged to pay for each of the six rooms in cash.

We were very wary of an unpredictable, venal side to Croatian society, even growing a little paranoid that this was part of some kind of grand move against us. Honestly, we had been driven a little nuts by this point.

So we figured we would do what we always did and keep on working. And, as the days went by, we didn't pick up on any hostility. The guys drank but didn't get drunk, slept well, and bothered nobody. Whatever their business was, they were doing it professionally. But nobody kept secrets for long in Zaton.

After a couple of weeks of chitchat, of getting to learn they all spoke some English, they volunteered information, which they said we needed to keep to ourselves. They were part of a police unit within the Ministry of the Interior. Their role was personal protection, and they had been assigned to duties in the area.

Over time we got to know that the man they were protecting was a judge recently involved in the case against former Dinamo Zagreb executive Zdravko Mamić. This was the man in Croatian football, who the night before the guilty verdict was delivered by the judge, got his ass out of Croatia.

The authorities had intelligence that someone had bankrolled a Mafioso-style hit on one of the judges. The cops had every reason to suspect the hit would be carried out if the judge could be tracked down. So someone in Zagreb decided to send him to the coast along with those nine armed bodyguards, all fanny packing heat.

The judge and his family were housed in a little property close to *The Admiral* and the bodyguards were on a rota to ensure it was guarded around the clock. Three of them would stay in the house with him each night while the other six stayed with us.

I asked one of the guys if he figured anything might come of this, and if he thought we were all safe. I told him we already had CCTV cameras, and that we were pretty security conscious. But obviously this mafia hit thing was on a different level. I mean, I was becoming seriously pregnant and the nesting instincts basically compelled me to ask if I should expect snipers or bombers or Russian poisoners or whatever to arrive at *The Admiral*.

He didn't seem too concerned and said they would handle any problems. I think he didn't want to say anything that might not sound good to a pregnant woman in case I kicked him and his team the hell out of *The Admiral*. Then he said he liked how the hotel staff were wearing the colors of the Croatian flag on our uniforms.

The biggest news story of the summer wasn't that Mamić had been found guilty and ran away to meet his money in Bosnia. That was the second biggest. The biggest was that the national soccer team was hammering ahead in the 2018 World Cup. If there was one thing more exciting to our staff than playing our little part in the Mamić story, it was that, in July, their team made its way to the finals of one of the biggest sporting events on the planet.

All of us, including the crew, who were incidentally from around Zaton and Sibenik, were kitted out in the red, white, and blue of Croatia for the duration of the competition.

We got ourselves an outdoor projector and showed all the Croatia matches under fine skies on the hotel terrace and screened pretty much every other game too. Guests and locals alike mingled and cheered and partied as the world played its heart out at the Russian venues. Croatians would set off fireworks each time the team scored, and loud little rockets blasted off into the sky over the bay.

In the end, it was France who took the trophy on the evening of July 15th, yet the thrill and excitement of our new country's progress infected everyone everywhere in the most upbeat and wonderful way. In that summer a whole community of tourists, locals, along with us Americans waved *trobojnica* (tricolor) flags and cheered on the team that spoke so well for a nation on the pitch.

Jonathan and I knew very little about soccer but in that hot summer of 2018, as a billion people watched the matches, we could say for sure we were Croatian fans through and through.

It was at times like those, when the place was full and the drinks and tacos and pizza were selling so well, that *The Admiral* really came into its own. The brilliant Dani sang classics on the weekend, Josip took our happy guests on boat trips every day, and the sun never failed to smile down on little Zaton.

It had been decades since the days when people came together at the old meeting house to dance and debate and plan in the time of Tito. And now, more than thirty years since he died from gangrene, it really felt reborn and beautiful, at the heart of the bay once more, loved again by a village which, regardless of history or politics, felt strongly that this building was very much their own.

This was more than we had hoped for, more than just designing and running a boutique hotel in a lovely place. We were lucky enough to find ourselves giving back by doing what we wanted to do.

We had a friend of Jonathan's work with us that summer. Daniel flew in from California to manage our crazy busy little restaurant *Konoba Kalifornja* because he had so much experience. He was dynamic in what he did, taking it to the next level, ensuring better, faster food, ever higher quality service.

We took on a young local woman, Kristina, to help run the front desk. Josipa was our rockstar of a maid, and our chefs were perfect in terms of delivering the menu we always hoped to have and Vinka and Daniel were managing the Konoba.

The hotel was running like clockwork, everything clicking into place when needed if not before. It felt as if everyone we met was buzzing about *The Admiral*. We even had to turn down bookings, put out more seats on the terrace, make more space in the bar, turn the rooms around faster, and buy in more stock than ever.

We got to know the local mayor, Boris, pretty well too. He liked to come over, to talk about how great it was that we were bringing people from all over the world to the village. He looked through the guest book and reviews, and saw our visitors were from South Africa, The Netherlands, Russia, UK, France, South America, Australia, Germany, France. He said he knew first timers were taking away great memories of days spent in Zaton and Dalmatia. He wanted to know how long we would be staying, what was the situation with the purchase of the hotel by Filip, and admitted he had some concerns as the future beyond the season seemed unclear.

We got to meet some of the bodyguards and noticed how they had become so relaxed as the weeks went on. We also noticed how pistols were appearing in the waistbands of shorts, rather than always being zipped tightly away in fanny packs. In fact, by this stage, Jonathan had clicked so well with these guys they had taken him to a shooting range after having a few beers in the bar.

One evening one of the bodyguards said he was surprised to hear there was no offer of an extension to our three-year contract. He said he had picked up on some local curiosity about what was going on, that he couldn't work it out. We said only that there was a lack of communication, that we expected if the lease was not updated we would be back in California in a few months, and that we weren't ready for that yet.

We said we had lost our shot at the hotel with the legal stuff. Our happy plan to own *The Admiral* ourselves, maybe lease it at some stage, maybe go on to design another *Admiral* somewhere else in Croatia, was a dead duck.

Bizarrely enough, the guy said he could have someone look into things, into Filip's background, and pass on anything he felt we might need to know. He felt it would be a shame if the village was to lose us.

Maybe it was because I was pregnant, but I shed some tears about that. Our hearts may have been smashed by the auctioneer's hammer, but we really just had to get used to the idea our world was changing.

It was a great season, but honestly being pregnant and working so many hours was desperately exhausting. I felt sometimes like I could sleep for a month if I had the chance, but I never got the chance. It didn't help that, in sleeping terms, a cafe/bar close to us called *Riva* started pumping out Euro techno until the wee hours.

It was only once a month so we could handle it, but those nights of non-stop thumping went all through the hotel until five in the morning and didn't help prove our pitch that Zaton was a piece of laid-back paradise.

The very worst thing was that one night the same track got stuck and played over and over until the sun came up. It got stuck or else the DJ was shit.

We got a few complaints from guests on those nights, which was understandable. We made a few complaints to the management of *Riva* but nothing came of it. Jonathan did talk to some of the kids who liked to gather in the square at one point after they had been there. They were, as usual, totally respectful, although pretty wasted. In fact, he once had to go out in the middle of the night to ask them to move on, to say people were trying to sleep. The kids apologized and walked quietly away.

It felt wrong to look back now and still feel a sense of dread about that summer because it was a truly special time, but that's the way it was. There was a genuine sense of uncertainty for Jonathan and me, and it was magnified given we had a baby coming into our lives. We literally didn't know where this kid would spend his earliest days. We had to be sure we could support our baby yet no longer knew if that meant staying put and working hard or if it would mean packing our bags. The decision to clear that up could only come from Filip.

We made a number of approaches and ended up meeting with him and his wife when they came to Croatia. They knew we were feeling the stress, that our efforts had been so big, our hopes so high, our outlay so extensive, and yet our future was just a blank. I know they knew of our stress because Filip's wife tried to give me a Xanax and said I should calm down. She said being pregnant was no time for tension. *No shit, lady.* From then on they were cold and some-what unreasonable.

We asked what they thought about us lining up another season for 2019 and they said that was not how they saw this going. We asked how they did see this going. The response was something along the lines of lets take things as they come.

We wondered if they were considering taking on new management, if they were thinking about running the place themselves.

We asked what the issue was with us running the hotel. Had we done something wrong?

We wondered how things were going to work with the rent now they had taken over. Should we expect it to change? When would we talk about that? And what about all the furniture and other goods we had bought? What about the staff? What about bookings being requested for the following season? What about all our social media promoting the place? They had politician answers for everything and wouldn't give us a straight answer.

We sent them an email just in case he didn't get it that we had a 9.3 (looking to finish this season as 9.4) on booking.com as well as a 4.5/5 and certificate of excellence from TripAdvisor.

But we got nowhere.

So the message, despite never being clarified, was that we were gone. When the season ended, technically in January 2019, we had to pack our bags. When we tried to raise the many residual issues, we heard nothing. And then, right out of the blue, a one liner.

I will pray for you.

"What the actual...?"

Jonathan wrote a handwritten letter after that. We were hoping that when Filip's prayer ended he might have the manners to talk with us.

We posted it on September 1st, 2018, two days before the unexpectedly early arrival of our son.

Filip and family,

We wanted to try and reach out one last time in order to try and move forward amicably. We would like to know how you would like us to handle the closure of the hotel and the removal of our items.

Since we have not heard from you or your attorney, we will continue to operate and finish our season. I still hope your prayers are with us as I am about to welcome my first child into the world any day. And with radio silence on your end it is creating a lot of unnecessary stress.

Simply put, an answer of your intention is all I have been praying for but nothing. As I said in my last email, we are willing to walk away and leave everything as it is - by selling you all the furnishings, fixtures, bookings and the list goes on - this will allow you to start the next season right away.

Having to dismantle everything we have built over the past three years and turn away all the business we have established for next season would truly be a shame. And that is why we are willing to hand it over at a fair price with depreciation on all items, equipment, and so forth.

Megan and I would just like to settle this so we can move on.

At this point we are not trying to change your mind - we have accepted that you want nothing to do with us as tenants - but at least have the decency to deal with us as human beings.

This is my last attempt at just trying to end things with no animosity on our side. We have no idea why you have put in so much effort to ignore us. Megan clearly deserves to know our future as she brings our son into the world.

In closing I wish nothing but the best for all of you and hope that whatever you do with the property brings together the community like The Admiral has done.

We hope you can answer us as to what you would like to do in terms of the operation of the property.

Regards, Jonathan Riff.

But the asshole didn't respond.

And, oh yeah, just in case we weren't already pissed off enough, right around this time our bank account got emptied and our cards stopped working.

EIGHTEEN

(Jonathan)

MY wife and I brought criminal charges against Karlo.
The contract, redrawn to reflect the reduction in rent after
our first season, had a convoluted addendum which his people
had enacted. It gave access to our finances in case we didn't pay
up.

As the legal wrangles over what had happened at the auction
were ongoing, the money we had deposited with the court was
returned to us. And then most of it went out again, straight to the
office of our former landlord.

We argued that not only were we in the dark about this
addendum (thanks, lawyers), but we were not even advised what
was happening when it began. We had been available to talk at
any time but heard nothing.

Karlo lost the property so had questionable right to charge rent on it. The hotel had been in the bank's hands for four years before that anyway, although we had to find that out for ourselves.

Karlo's people said, through lawyers, that we owed the money to him for 2018 no matter what. They said that the ownership issue wasn't technically a done deal so *The Admiral* was still in his hands. So that's why the money got pulled from our account. All €80,000 {$95,000} of it.

Given we were hearing nothing from Filip and that Karlo had sold up, and given that the bank held the deeds anyway, we felt like rag dolls getting thrown around and torn up, victims of everyone else's dispute.

Karlo showed no willingness to enter into any discussion in terms of giving the money back. His bullshit addendum was only tacked on in the first place because, as he accepted, the initial rent demand was too high. It was maddening. And the legal advice didn't help. All we were told was that we were looking at a long, drawn out fight to get our money back.

Megan called Karlo's office. She was crying her eyes out. She talked about our baby and said we were at the end of a rope, and said she couldn't believe what had happened. I remember very clearly Megan saying, "You don't have a heart." Mine broke a little when I heard it. Neither Karlo nor anyone connected with him did anything to help.

All this stuff had been going on right when Megan was about to give birth, right when she needed to be sure she was doing all she could to have a healthy baby. It's not as if we didn't already have plenty to worry about.

A doctor we had visited in Šibenik had not been good for us. Way back at the start of her pregnancy there was an initial scan. Then we sat down with that doctor. She looked over the ultrasound image, and with a straight face, told us she expected Megan would have a miscarriage. When, filling up with questions and emotion, we asked why, she said only that the picture didn't look right. She said she had no doubt what was going to happen, that we would have to get ready.

That doctor was wrong. And also, without any doubt, was a terrible human being. People we told about that were horrified. We were swamped with support and recommendations for doctors, mid wives, nannies, and others who knew the emotional and physical journey of the pregnancy process.

Josip was great during all that. His wife was pregnant at the same time and he sympathized hard. He could not have done more to help, to keep trying to take work off our hands. He took Megan to the hospital for two appointments so he could help out with translation, making sure she understood everything that was going on.

He said that the doctor who said that unfounded, nasty bullshit about a miscarriage had an attitude that did not represent his country. That she should be ashamed. He was right too. A pregnant woman really does get treated with great respect in Croatia, really gets put on a pedestal, as Megan found out. It's something that brings out the best in the place. A lot of the best came out in Zaton right through her pregnancy because a total of seven women in the village were pregnant at the same time. I guess it was something to do with that long cold winter.

We took advice from Dani and Ante in terms of the medical matters and trekked to Zagreb for the best treatment we could get. A doctor examined Megan thoroughly and told us a healthy little boy would be joining us in the fall.

Through all of that, Daniel really went out of his way to run the whole hotel by himself, to manage not just the restaurant but everything else too, to make sure we had as little to worry about as possible. Kristina was helping out as well, handling bookings, dealing with guest issues.

As the season drew to a close in September the bodyguards, like the tourists, began moving out one by one. They told us many times they had enjoyed their summer in Zaton. They said they were sorry to hear that this was it for us. Those guys never did look into the circumstances around who was involved in the rotten auction. We never pushed them to do so, never felt that would be a good idea.

But it was comforting to know that, at least to some extent, they had our back.

The tourists began to leave, the hotel got a little emptier, the days got a little shorter, the smell from the bay got a little worse. Pretty soon our little family of Megan, Sailor, River, our imminent arrival and I were waving off the last guests we would host. Megan was too pregnant to think about flying home, too downbeat to want to go anywhere. I was pissed off, trying to make the finances work, trying to figure out how bad it all was, to work out when we should go home, where we would go when we got there, what the hell we would do.

We figured we should just get ourselves to Zagreb, rent a little place and wait for our son to arrive. Our dogs were eating each other up at the time and Dani and Ante kindly took in River so we could get through the new baby days ahead.

I guess we got pretty enraged when, as our world became all about that little boy, we got word via Filip's lawyer. We were instructed to lock up the hotel as soon as we could, to leave everything inside just as it was. We were told to take nothing with us but our personal effects because Filip owned it all. He would, we were told, come after us if anything went missing. All we should do was walk away, the lawyer said, and forever end our connection with *The Admiral*.

Just leave quietly, in other words.

Yeah, right.

NINETEEN

Croatia Journal: Franjo Tudman Airport, Zagreb. March 2019.

WE called him Roko, a gorgeous little Croatian name for a gorgeous little Croatian born boy. He was born close to midnight on Labor Day just after a mighty storm had rolled over Zagreb.

We took him home to California when he was six months old. We couldn't wait to introduce him to the magnificent Pacific coast, to the whole United States of America. We were leaving this astonishing country for the last time and returning to our own.

He was named after the saint whose name is carried by the little church right beside The Admiral. Roko means to roar or a battle cry and that makes sense to us. So much about our journey had not made sense to us. Roko was only six months old and we laughed when we think how, even at that age, he made more sense to us than the last three infuriating, exasperating, incredible years.

We'd been staying in a little house in the hills outside Zagreb and getting to know our little guy. We'd been looking at ideas for what we might do when we got back. Our visas were done anyway so we had no choice but to go. And we were officially bankrupt too. Everything we had was gone. It's not how we wanted to leave that place, but on the upside no one can get any more money from us.

Filip's lawyer made it clear he wanted us gone by the end of 2018, that there was nothing to discuss. Filip, we were told, owned everything in the building. We must leave empty handed. We reached a point, after Roko was born, where we came to terms with it all, where we just said *jebiga* to ourselves, where we decided to call it a day.

So we got to thinking of ways to say goodbye to everything, to Croatia, to the people of Zaton, to our hotel. We knew our lawyer was against what we ended up doing and advised it was against the law. He said that in order to clean our books we should avoid doing it. But honestly, truly, totally, we no longer gave a fuck.

With the help of a few wonderful friends, we got ourselves some price tags and walked from room to room through *The Admiral*, from bar to lobby, from attic to terrace, from kitchen to bathrooms.

We marked those tickets as low as we could go, turned our hotel into the biggest bargain basement sale in Dalmatia. We put the word around, called on villagers to come see if any of the fine things in our hotel would suit them. And they did. In numbers.

We sold the bedsheets, the spoons, the lamps, the chairs, the CCTV cameras and air-con units. Over three days we sold alcohol and televisions, fridges and rugs. We even sold the bits and pieces which made up the nautical rope and copper bar closets which the tourism minister hated so much.

We sold hats and toiletries and towels and plates and the coffee machine in the bar, the pizza oven in the kitchen. We sold the boat, the bicycles, the paintings, the shampoo, the cocktail shakers, and part of the floor.

Staff took pieces with our compliments as we told them we were sorry at how it had all worked out. We saw most of the people who had worked for us, although we didn't ever see Kristina again.

We gave a queen-size bed and mattress to our dear pizza chef, Geza, who had suffered from sleeping and comfort problems in the past. She held Roko close to her full breasts as we helped move it for her. He fell asleep and she said he was so comfortable there. That to him her boobs were 'like clouds'. We wished Geza only the deepest of sleeps and sweetest of dreams too.

As the big sale came to a close, as all of what Filip claimed to own went walking right out the door and into the lovely homes of Zaton, the reality of what was taking place hit home. Villagers we barely knew were arriving to shake our hands, to give us hugs, to say we would be missed.

The staff of *Porat*, some of the guys from the harbor, and the kids in the square all said they were sad to see us go. Mayor Boris advised us this was a loss for the village, local influencer Çoga said he was disappointed, our tiler Branko and our electrician Romeo sent word it was a sad day.

All we could do was hold up little Roko, take him around the gutted inside of the hotel we had once filled with happy guests, and tell him that the place would always be so special in the hearts of his mom and dad.

In Zagreb, on our last days there, Josip arrived exhausted at the door of our rented house. He had volunteered to bring up the old Land Rover Defender which we had left at the side of the hotel. It had broken down just one street away and Josip had tried to push it the rest of the way. We were amazed it had even gotten that far. We knew that Karlo's people had always wanted that old vehicle and, as a way of sending out a farewell message, we made sure they never got it.

Josip's son was born around the same time as ours. We talked for a while about our little boys, but we knew he wouldn't hang around in Zagreb for long. He explained to us before how true Dalmatians had little time for the capital, that all he wanted to do whenever he was there was go home. So he turned away, headed for the door.

We told him that was it, that we would be going in a few days.

He wished us all the greatest with Roko and we said the same.

He said, just like a fun fact about Croatia, that all the seven simultaneous pregnancies of Zaton in 2018 had resulted in boys. Our fun fact for Josip was that he was the best guy to have on our team, that he was the greatest representative of Croatia. We said he had always been there on our best days, and was always willing to help out on our worst.

So Sailor was put in her box and taken away for the long trip home after three years away. We knew she'd forgive us in time, that she'd blend back into the US lifestyle just fine.

We had a lot of goodbyes to say and it hadn't been easy, hadn't been how we would have wanted it to be. But it was time to say goodbye to it all.

TWENTY

USA. 2021.

BONUS fun facts about Croatia?
Shakespeare's *Twelfth Night* comedy play was set in Dalmatia. Per capita, they say Croatia is fourth in the world for alcohol consumption.

The longest strudel in history was baked there, coming in at 1,479.38 meters.

The whole country is slightly smaller than West Virginia.

Also a fact - we never did learn to speak the language fluently but we could figure out what was being said and we knew all about their moms.

Legal matters dragged on, and who knows if we'll ever get any money back.

What actually took place out there still hurts sometimes, still confuses us, still seems so unnecessary.

We often felt watched, distrusted, hamstrung, and even unwelcome at times, yet we also really did make a dream come true, really did take it as far as we could. We really did make some precious friends and, despite it all, we really did have the time of our lives.

We wonder how things would have been if we'd been allowed to continue on our journey. Would it have been better for Zaton if we had kept bringing tourists there, kept promoting and adoring Dalmatia and Croatia, kept on living and loving there with our little boy and happy dogs into the years ahead?

Was it better that a great little hotel with its stream of five-star reviews was shut down without explanation? Was it better that tourists were told they wouldn't be able to stay there in the season ahead because Filip had no operating plans in place? Was it better that after uprooting our lives to do something special in Zaton, we had to leave a village that was so dear to us?

Or was this the best way everything could have panned out? Megan always said it happened for a reason and with the outbreak of Covid I finally agreed with her.

The hotel has yet to reopen. Its doors have been locked, its rooms, kitchen, lobby, bar and terrace have been silent since we left it in 2019. We heard a while ago that our former landlord had come calling on the shut down building just to see what was left in there. Karlo was seen trying to secure a few leftover items, to collect a few more bits and pieces for his collection. Such a shame he didn't get the Defender.

Local people and tourists alike stroll past *The Admiral* these days as they take in the bay. We think sometimes some among them might look over and wonder what it would be like to reopen that old building, to turn it into an amazing boutique hotel, to live and work and love somewhere so beautiful.

We think about all that sometimes and say to ourselves, *What a waste.*

We found a new place to live for our strong family and dog. We're both back in the swing of things, still adjusting to our new lives back in the states and making things work, while still traveling as much as we can.

We're back now watching the big sun slip down into the horizon like we used to do, back getting pictures with Sailor in the countryside, getting pictures with Roko on the beach.

We are in love and once again in charge of our own lives.

We are strong and free and making a future in which we hope to make beautiful things, in which we give our boy the best childhood we can.

THE END

THE ADMIRAL - GUESTBOOK

Thank you for the wonderful stay in such a wonderful place. Everything was perfect, every time again.

..enjoyed everything; friendly staff, good beds and shower and tasty breakfast. Thanks!

The hotel is stunning and the staff fantastic.

The Admiral is a great place. You have made it a dream come true.

We love it. We love Zaton. We love The Admiral.

Thank you for the amazing time we spent here. You're awesome.

The hotel made it possible we could lay our heads on the best pillows.

Very kind crew, good rooms and price. Lovely little village.

Thanks for the lovely stay. We had a very nice moment.

Everything is so nicely arranged and charming.

Very comfy beds!!

Unbelievable location. What luck to have found it!

Only luck brought us here. We are such lucky people.

You are the greatest team we have ever met in the hotel industry. We were really happy to be your guests. If you ever visit St Petersburg...

Sailor is the cutest.

You have made something very special...

Love the interior, love the owners, love the staff and location is perfect... good luck with all your dreams, may they all come true.

The hotel - with all the little details - was wonderful. Have an amazing wedding.

We had an unforgettable time in Zaton.

By chance we came across The Admiral and were immediately smitten.

Beaucoup do charm...

Thanks to Josip who made our island hopping unforgettable.

I love Konoba Kalifornja... amazing little details around the hotel that tie everything together. The Admiral will always hold a very special place in my heart.

Your love truly shines for each other.

Your oasis is beautiful.

...best place we have been in Croatia.

You made everything so easy.

We knew when there was room at The Admiral it was meant to be that we go to Croatia.

...vibrant, daring and a dream that is so alive.